Collins
English for Exams

Cambridge English Qualifications

B1 Preliminary

Four Practice Tests

Collins

HarperCollins Publishers
The News Building
1 London Bridge Street
London
SE1 9GF

First edition 2014
10 9 8 7 6 5 4
© HarperCollins Publishers 2014
ISBN 978-0-00-752955-1
Collins® is a registered trademark of HarperCollins Publishers Limited
www.collinselt.com
A catalogue record for this book is available from the British Library
Typeset in India by Aptara
Printed and bound in China by RR Donnelley APS

Author: Peter Travis
Illustrators: Aptara
Audio recordings by Dsound

Photo credits

p26: **Cheryl Savan**/Shutterstock; p26: **Andresr**/Shutterstock; p26: **Tracy Whiteside**/Shutterstock; p26: **RyFlip**/Shutterstock; p26: **Rob Marmion**/Shutterstock; p32: **Teletrebi**/Shutterstock; p46: **Christin Slavkov**/Shutterstock; p46: **Darryl Brooks**/Shutterstock; p46: **Andresr**/Shutterstock; p46: **Martin Allinger**/Shutterstock; p46: **YanLev**/Shutterstock; p50: **Vladyslav Starozhylov**/Shutterstock; p52: **bajinda**/Shutterstock; p68: **Santhosh Kumar**/Shutterstock; p68: **michaeljung**/Shutterstock; p68: **eurobanks**/Shutterstock; p68: **Djomas**/Shutterstock; p68: **Oleg Golovnev**/Shutterstock; p74: **Dancing Fish**/Shutterstock; p88: **aastock**/Shutterstock; p88: **EDHAR**/Shutterstock; p94: **Lisa F. Young**/Shutterstock; p88: **Laurin Rinder**/Shutterstock; p88: **c12**/Shutterstock; p94: **Bill Perry**/Shutterstock; pii: **Surkov Vladimir**/Shutterstock; pii: **Blend Images**/Shutterstock; piv: **auremar**/Shutterstock; piv: **Iuliia Gusakova**/Shutterstock; pvi: **Kzenon**/Shutterstock; pvi: **Fotokostic**/Shutterstock; pviii: **wong sze yuen**/Shutterstock; pviii: **dotshock**/Shutterstock.

Contents

Introduction

About this book

Who is this book for?

This book will help you to prepare for the *Cambridge English Qualifications B1 Preliminary*. The exam was previously known as the *Preliminary English Test* or *PET*. This book will be useful if you are preparing for the exam for the first time or taking it again. The book and online training module have been designed so that you can use them to study on your own. However, you can also use the book if you are preparing for the *Cambridge English Qualifications B1 Preliminary* in a class.

Content

The book contains:

- **Tips for success** – important advice to help you to do well in the exam
- **Overview of *Cambridge English Qualifications B1 Preliminary*** – a guide to the exam
- **Quick guides** – easy-to-read guides to the different parts of each paper and summaries of what you need to know in order to answer the questions correctly
- **Challenges and solutions** – advice to help you to deal with common problems in each paper
- **Practice tests** – four complete practice tests
- **Mini-dictionary** – entries of difficult words from the practice tests in this book (these are from Collins COBUILD dictionaries)
- **Audio script** – the texts of what you hear in the Listening and Speaking papers
- **Sample answer sheets** – make sure you know what the answer sheets for the Reading and Writing and Listening papers look like
- **Answer key** – the answers for the Reading section of the Reading and Writing papers as well as the Listening papers
- **Model answers** – examples of good answers for the questions in the Writing section of the Reading and Writing papers as well as the Speaking papers
- **CD** – MP3 files with all the recordings for the practice tests as well as model answers for the Speaking papers
- **Access code for online training module** - online practice tests with help and advice to help you improve your skills

Tips for success

Make a plan to succeed and start by following these tips.

- **Register for the test early** – If you are studying on your own, use the Cambridge Assessment English website to find your local exam centre. Register as early as you can to give yourself lots of time to prepare.
- **Start studying early** – The more you practise, the better your English will become. Give yourself at least one month to revise and complete all the practice tests in this book. Spend at least one hour a day studying.
- **Time yourself** when you do the practice tests. This will help you to feel more confident when you do the real exam.
- **Do every part** of each practice test. Don't be afraid to make notes in the book. For example, writing down the meaning of words you don't know on the page itself will help you to remember them later on.
- In the Writing section, **keep practising until you can write a full answer** within the time limit.

Using the book for self-study

If you haven't studied for the *Cambridge English Qualifications B1 Preliminary* before, it is a good idea to do all the tests in this book in order. If you have a teacher or friend who can help you with your speaking and writing, that would be very useful. It is also a good idea to meet up with other students who are preparing for the exam or who want to improve their English. Having a study partner will help you to stay motivated. You can also help each other with areas of English you might find difficult.

Begin preparing for the *Cambridge English Qualifications B1 Preliminary* exam by getting to know the different parts of each paper, what each part tests and how many marks there are for each part. Use the information in this introduction as well as the *Quick guides* to find out all you can. You can also download the *Cambridge English Qualifications B1 Preliminary Handbook* from the Cambridge Assessment English website for more details. There is a link to the website below.

You need to know how to prepare for each of the papers in the best way possible. The *Challenges and solutions* section of this book will be useful. Try to follow the advice in it as it will help you to develop the skills you need.

When you are ready to try the practice tests, make sure you do the tasks in the Writing section of the Reading and Writing papers as well as the Speaking papers. You can only improve your skills by practising a lot. Practise writing to a time limit. If you find this difficult at first, start by writing a very good answer of the correct length without worrying about time. Then try to complete the tasks faster until you can write a good answer within the time limit. Learn to estimate the number of words you have written without counting them. Study the model answers at the back of the book. This will give you a clear idea of the standard your answers need to be. Don't try to memorise letters or stories for the Writing section or answers to the questions in the Speaking paper. If you work your way through the book, you should develop the skills and language you need to give good answers in the real exam.

Finally, read as much as possible in English; this is the best way to learn new vocabulary and improve your English.

Online training module

You can also prepare for the test online by working through the online training module. The training module contains two of the tests from the book. You can take one of the tests in 'test mode' and one of the tests in 'training mode'. The training module gives you tips and advice to help you improve your skills. There is additional practice material, so that you can work on areas you find difficult. The training module will help you prepare for both the paper-based test and the computer-based test.

For information on how to access the training module, please turn to the back of the book.

About *Cambridge English Qualifications B1 Preliminary*

Who is *Cambridge English Qualifications B1 Preliminary* for?

Cambridge English Qualifications B1 Preliminary is an intermediate-level English exam run by Cambridge Assessment English, also known as Cambridge ESOL. It is for people who need to show that they can deal with everyday English at an intermediate level. In other words, you have to be able to:

- understand the main points of simple instructions and public announcements.
- ask questions and take part in discussions about factual subjects.
- write emails, letters or notes.
- deal with most of the situations you might meet if you were a tourist in an English-speaking country.

The level of *Cambridge English Qualifications B1 Preliminary*

The exam is one of those offered by Cambridge Assessment English:

- Cambridge English C2 Proficiency
- Cambridge English C1 Advanced
- Cambridge English B2 First
- **Cambridge English B1 Preliminary**
- Cambridge English A2 Key

The table below shows how *Cambridge English Qualifications B1 Preliminary* fits into the Cambridge Assessment English Main Suite examinations. The level of *Cambridge English Qualifications B1 Preliminary* is described as being at B1 on the Common European Framework of Reference.

Proficient User	C2 Proficiency
	C1 Advanced
Independent user	B2 First
	B1 Preliminary
Basic User	A2 Key
	A1

The papers of *Cambridge English Qualifications B1 Preliminary*

There are three papers in the exam.

- Paper 1: Reading and Writing (1 hour and 30 minutes)
- Paper 2: Listening (30 minutes, plus 6 minutes for transferring answers to the answer sheet)
- Paper 3: Speaking (10–12 minutes)

Timetabling

Papers 1 and 2 must be taken on the same day, with Paper 1 first, followed by Paper 2. Paper 3 can be taken several days before or after the other papers. If you are studying on your own, you should contact your exam centre for dates. You can take the exam on computer or as a paper-based exam.

Marking

Each of the four skills (Reading, Writing, Listening and Speaking) is worth 25% of the total mark.

The **Reading** section of the Reading and Writing paper has 35 questions. There is one mark for each correct answer.

The **Writing** section of the Reading and Writing paper has seven questions.
In Part 1, there are five questions. There is one mark for each correct answer.
In Part 2, question 6 has five marks. You will get full marks only if you answer all three parts of the question and if you make only a few spelling or grammar mistakes.
In Part 3, question 7/8 has a total of 20 marks:

- five marks if you include all the necessary information
- five marks if you express your message clearly
- five marks if you organise your message so a reader can follow it easily
- five marks if you use a good range of grammar structures and vocabulary

The **Listening** paper has 25 questions. There is one mark for each correct answer

In the **Speaking** paper, you have to show you can:

- communicate and interact with the examiner and the other candidate
- pronounce words clearly
- organise language when you are speaking about something at length
- use a good range of grammar and vocabulary

These are the grades that can be awarded.

- Pass: 70% (approximately)
- Pass with Merit: 85% (approximately)
- Pass with Distinction: 90% (approximately)

If you get a Pass with Distinction, you will be awarded a *Cambridge English Qualifications B1 Preliminary* certificate stating that you have shown ability at Level B2. If you score below 70%, you could be awarded a certificate at Level A2.

For more information on how the test is marked, go to:
http://www.cambridgeenglish.org

Guide to *Cambridge English Qualifications B1 Preliminary*

Quick guide

What is it?

The Reading section of *Paper 1: Reading and Writing* tests how well you can understand general English texts. It includes different types of texts about lots of different subjects.

Skills needed

In order to do well in the Reading section, you must be able to:
- read real-world texts such as emails, signs and articles and understand the main ideas, details the writer's opinion and his / her reason for writing scan some text to find a particular piece of information.
- answer questions within the given time.

The Reading section

The Reading section has five parts.

Part 1 has five short real-world texts, for example, notices, messages, emails and signs and five questions. You have to read each text and choose the correct answer from three options, A, B or C. (Total marks: 5)

Part 2 has five short descriptions of people and eight short texts. You have to match each of the descriptions with the right text. (Total marks: 5)

Part 3 has a longer text and ten statements. You have to decide if the statements are correct or incorrect. (Total marks: 10)

Part 4 has a longer text and five multiple-choice questions. You have to understand details about the text as well as the writer's attitude, opinion on a particular issue and his/her purpose for writing. (Total marks: 5)

Part 5 has a short text with ten gaps. You have to fill the gaps by choosing the correct word from four options, A, B, C or D. (Total marks: 10)

Challenges and solutions

» **CHALLENGE 1: 'I don't know a lot of the words that I see in the texts or in the questions.'**

SOLUTION: Build your vocabulary. Start by downloading the *Cambridge English Qualifications B1 Preliminary* Vocabulary List from the Cambridge Assessment English website. This is a list of words that you should understand. Look through the list and

not know. Then look up their meaning in a dictionary. Knowing these words will help you to do better in the test.

SOLUTION: Use a learner's dictionary when you study. Dictionaries such as the *Collins COBUILD Illustrated Intermediate Dictionary of English* have clear definitions, example sentences, information about grammar and illustrations to help you to build your vocabulary. At the back of this book, there is a mini-dictionary with definitions of difficult words. The definitions come from Collins COBUILD.

SOLUTION: Use 'key' words and phrases that appear before and after unknown words to help you guess their meaning. Read the sentence with the unknown word carefully. You may also need to read the whole paragraph in order to work out the meaning. In the table below there are some ideas for how key words and phrases might help you to understand a word. The unknown word is underlined.

Guessing the meaning of unknown words		
Ideas	**Key words and phrases**	**Examples**
Pay attention to examples near the unknown word. If you understand the examples, you can use them to guess the meaning of the unknown word.	*such as* *including* *this includes* *like* *for instance* *for example*	*The students had different* <u>*excuses*</u> *for not doing their homework,* **such as** *'My dog ate it' or 'My mum washed it in the washing machine'.*
Look for key words that show the writer is contrasting two ideas. The unknown word might have the opposite meaning to the idea expressed in the sentence before or after it.	*but* *while* *Unlike X, . . .* *On the other hand, X . . .* *However, . . .*	*There is going to be a heat* <u>*wave*</u> *all this week.* **However***, the weather will be much colder next week.*

SOLUTION: Look at parts of words such as prefixes and suffixes to guess the meaning of unknown words. A prefix is one or more letters, *e.g. un-, dis-, pre-, co-,* under-, that go at the beginning of a word, e.g. <u>un</u>happy, <u>dis</u>organised. A suffix is one or more letters, e.g. *-ful, -less, -ation, -y, -ment, -hood,* that go at the end of a word, e.g. *enjoy<u>ment</u>, neighbour<u>hood</u>*. If you learn the meanings of common English prefixes and suffixes, you will be able to guess the meaning of many unknown words. For example, the prefixes *un-* and *dis-* give a word a negative meaning.

» **CHALLENGE 2: 'I often don't have enough time to finish all of the questions.'**

SOLUTION: Read the text quickly using skimming and scanning skills to find the answers to questions. Skimming is when you read a text quickly, paying attention only to the most important ideas. In this way, you can often quickly find the important sections that many questions are based on. This will save you a lot of time. To be good at skimming, make sure you know where to find the most important ideas in a text. In the table below there is some information on where to find important ideas.

Part of the text	Skimming strategy
Titles/Headings	Read the title of a text; this sometimes gives you an idea of what the text is about. In the same way, paragraph headings may help you to find the topic of each paragraph.
Introduction	Read the last two or three sentences of the introductory paragraph. They often include the main idea of the text.
Main paragraphs	Read the first and last sentence of a paragraph. They usually include the main idea of the paragraph.
Conclusion	Read the first two or three sentences of the conclusion. They often say in a few words what the text was about.

Scanning is when you read a text quickly in order to find specific key words or ideas. After you have read a question and its answer options, you should make a note of any key words or ideas such as names or numbers. Then scan the text, looking specifically for those key words or ideas. The answers appear in the texts in the same order as the questions so if you have found the part of the text that answers a question, the part of the text that answers the next question must be below that part.

You do not need to understand every word when you skim or scan a text. The most important thing is to find the information you need in order to answer the questions quickly and correctly.

To practise skimming and scanning, find an article in a newspaper or magazine. First, skim the article and write down the most important ideas on a piece of paper. Then scan it for key words or ideas such as names or numbers. The more you practise skimming and scanning, the better you will become so try to practise every day.

SOLUTION: Time yourself when you do practice tests. You should not spend more than 50 minutes on the Reading section and you should try to allow more time for Parts 3, 4 and 5 as the texts and questions in them are more difficult than those in Parts 1 and 2. While you work on the questions, be sure to look at your watch occasionally. Do not spend too long on any one question; if you cannot answer it, carry on to the next question and go back to it later. This will help you to not get stuck on a question and waste your time.

» **CHALLENGE 3: 'None of the multiple choice answer options "feel" right.'**

SOLUTION: Make sure you understand the question types in each part of the paper and the skills you need to answer them. The same question types appear in every Reading and Writing paper. If you know which skills each part tests, you will avoid surprises in the real test and you will be able to answer the questions with more confidence.

SOLUTION: Decide which answer options are clearly incorrect. Usually, you can ignore an option that has:

- information that is the opposite of the facts in the text.
- information that does not answer the question.

SOLUTION: If you find that you are spending too much time on one question and you are not sure of the answer, move on to the next question or the next part. If you have time, you can return to it later. Some people find it easier to answer difficult questions once they have had time to think about them.

SOLUTION: Find evidence for your answer in the text. For example, if you think option A is correct, find the part of the text where the answer is and underline it. Make sure you are not just matching words in the question to words in the text and be careful that the answer is correct as a whole. This is important in Part 2, where you have to match people with descriptions; a description may have some of the information but not all of it.

» CHALLENGE 4: 'I find it difficult to identify the writer's opinion in Part 4.'

SOLUTION: In this part, you have to understand general points about the text and not just particular facts. You might be asked why the writer wrote the text or what his/her opinion is on a subject. These questions are always the first and the last (questions 21 and 25). Try answering these last. By the time you have answered the other questions, you will have a better understanding of the whole text and be in a better position to answer these more general questions.

SOLUTION: Read lots of articles in magazines and newspaper reports. Do not worry about understanding every word; the articles will be at a higher level than the ones you are used to. Practise trying to get a general idea of what the articles are about and why the writer has written them.

» CHALLENGE 5: 'I find it hard to decide what the missing word is in Part 5.'

SOLUTION: Some gaps need a 'grammar' word. These are words such as determiners (e.g. *a, the, much, many*), prepositions (e.g. *on, at, in*) and conjunctions (e.g. *and, but, because*). Make a list of all the types of grammar words you find in practice tests and learn them so you understand how they are used.

SOLUTION: Work with a partner and make your own text with gaps. Find a short text and cross out grammar words. Then create four answer options for each gap.

SOLUTION: Some gaps need words that are part of a set expression. For example, a text might have the expressions *at least* and *spend time*, and *at* and *spend* are in the gaps. Focus on the words around a gap and decide if the missing word is part of a set expression. Make a list of vocabulary 'chunks' like these and not just individual words.

SOLUTION: Skip the gaps you do not know and come back to them later. Cross out the answer options that you know are wrong so you have fewer options to choose from.

Quick guide

What is it?

The Writing section of Paper 1 Reading and Writing tests how well you can write an answer to a question using a good range of vocabulary and grammatical structures.

Skills needed

In order to do well in the Writing section, you must be able to:

- understand the instructions and identify the key points that you have to include in your answer.
- use a good range of B1-level vocabulary and grammatical structures.
- write texts such as postcards, letters, notes and emails.
- write a well-organised text that is easy for the reader to follow.
- rephrase information given in the instructions.
- write your answers within the word limits given in the instructions.
- write your answers within the given time.

The Writing section

The Writing section has three parts.

Part 1 tests your grammar. It has five questions. Each question has a pair of sentences. The second sentence in each pair has a gap. You have to complete the gap with one, two or three words so that the second sentence has the same meaning as the first sentence. (Total marks: 5)

Part 2 tests how well you can communicate information clearly. You will need to write a short message (35–44 words) such as an email or note. The instructions ask you to include three important points in your message. (Total marks: 5)

Part 3 tests how well you can communicate, organise your ideas and use a range of language. This part gives you a choice of two different tasks: a letter or a short story. Your answer must be about 100 words. In order to write the letter, you have to read part of a letter from a friend and reply, For the short story, you are given a title or sentence which you have to use at the beginning of your answer. (Total marks: 20)

Challenges and solutions

» **CHALLENGE 1: 'I'm not sure how much time to spend on each question.'**

SOLUTION: Know how much time you have. On the day of the exam, wear a watch. While you work, keep an eye on the time. Use this guide while you write.

Part 1: 10 minutes	
Time	**What you should do**
1 minute	Read the instructions carefully and look through the questions quickly.
7 minutes	Complete the sentences. Do the easy ones first.
2 minutes	Check your answers carefully.
Part 2: 10 minutes	
1 minute	Read the instructions carefully. Underline the key words in each of the three points.
7 minutes	Write your answer. Make sure you answer all three points. Think about how you can express the ideas in the points using different words and/or structures.
2 minutes	Check your spelling and watch out for mistakes in your grammar.
Part 3: 20 minutes	
2 minutes	Read the instructions carefully. Decide which question you are going to answer. If you choose the letter, underline the key words in the instructions.
2 minutes	Make notes and plan your answer. Think about a good beginning, middle and end.
14 minutes	Write your answer.
2 minutes	Check your spelling and watch out for mistakes in your grammar.

SOLUTION: Practise writing within a time limit before the real exam. Start by giving yourself 15 minutes more than the time limit in the exam and slowly cut this until you can finish writing a few minutes early. You will need this time to read through your work to check for mistakes.

» **CHALLENGE 2: 'I'm afraid that the examiner won't understand the ideas in my writing.'**

SOLUTION: Use linking words. Linking words connect two sentences or clauses together. They work like signs on a road and show the reader where you are going in your text; they make it easier to understand. In the table below there are some useful linking words and expressions. Add new words or expressions as you learn them.

Use	Examples
To show the order of events	*First, ...* *At the beginning, ...* *Then ...* *After that, ...* *Next, ...* *Finally, ...* *In the end, ...*
To contrast two points	*but* *although* *However, ...*

To give examples	for example for instance like such as
To give more information, to add	and also In addition, ...

SOLUTION: Practise your spelling. A few misspelled words will not affect your score but a lot of spelling mistakes may stop the examiner from understanding your meaning. One way to improve your spelling is to read a lot; the more often you see words in English, the more easily you will learn how common words are spelled.

SOLUTION: What are your spelling problems? Do you sometimes forget to add *-s* to plural nouns? Do you forget that some adjectives change when they are in the comparative form (e.g. *heavy – heavier, hot – hotter*)? Maybe you have difficulty remembering the past forms of irregular verbs. Make a list of your spelling problems and always check your work for these.

SOLUTION: Make sure your handwriting is easy to read. It does not matter if you use capital letters all the time and you do not have to join the letters together within words. But you should be confident that other people can understand your handwriting. Ask a friend to read some of your work and then tell you if it is clear or if any letters or words are difficult to read.

» **CHALLENGE 3: 'I don't know how to re-write the sentences in Part 1.'**

SOLUTION: When you do Part 1, think about possible language you might be tested on. For example, you may be asked to change an active sentence to a passive sentence, or put direct speech into indirect speech.

Active:	*My son wrote this book.* →
Passive:	*This book <u>was written</u> by my son.*
Direct speech:	*'Do you mind closing the window?' the woman asked the man.* →
Indirect speech:	*The woman asked the man <u>to close</u> the window.*

Each time you do a practice test, keep a record of the language that was tested. You will soon notice that certain structures are tested very often.

SOLUTION: An easy way to remember the different patterns in Part 1 is to use them to describe you or your experiences. For example, here is a typical Part 1 question:

Judy moved to London three years ago. →
It is three years .... Judy moved to London.
The missing word is *since*. The sentences below might describe you:
I started my English course six months ago. →
It is six months since I started my English course.

» **CHALLENGE 4: 'I find it difficult to write notes or emails.'**

SOLUTION: There are many words and phrases that native speakers use in letters or emails. If you can remember these words and phrases, you will find it easier to start your piece of writing and bring it to an end. In the table below there are some examples. Add new ones as you learn them.

Section of message	Set expressions
Beginning	*How are you?* *I hope you're well.* *Thanks for your letter.* *It was great to hear from you.*
Commenting on information you have received	*I'm sorry to hear …* *I'm / I was so pleased to hear …* *It's / It was great to hear …*
Ending	*Write back soon.* *Best wishes* *See you soon.* *Take care.*

SOLUTION: Keep a record of examples of the informal language you can use in emails or letters. In the table below there are some examples. Add new ones as you learn them.

	Informal	Formal
Contractions	*I'm / You're / It's got*	*I am / You are / It has got*
Vocabulary	*Hiya.* *Brilliant!*	*Hello.* *Very good!*
Grammar	Active	Passive
Punctuation	Lots of exclamation marks (!)	Exclamation marks only when absolutely necessary

» **CHALLENGE 5: 'I'm not sure how to improve my vocabulary for the exam.'**

SOLUTION: The Part 2 task might ask you to thank someone, to suggest something or to apologise about something. Make sure you record useful words and phrases to do these things. In the table below there are some examples. Add new ones as you learn them.

Function	Expressions
Thanking	*Many thanks for …* *Thanks very much for …*
Suggesting	*Why don't you …?* *What about …?* *Try …*
Apologising	*I'm sorry but …* *Apologies but …*

SOLUTION: Practise paraphrasing (= saying the same things using different words). Find a reading text from the Reading section of this book. Then choose a paragraph and read it carefully. Close the book and try saying what you have read by paraphrasing. When you have finished, compare your paragraph with the one in the book. Did you change key words by using synonyms (= words with the same meaning)? Did you change structures (e.g. active to passive)? Practise paraphrasing one paragraph a day until you feel confident about your paraphrasing skills.

» **CHALLENGE 6: 'I don't know how to write a good story for the Part 3 question.'**

SOLUTION: If you have trouble thinking of something to write about in a story, use question words to help you think of ideas. Ask yourself questions beginning with *where, when, who and why*. Imagine you have to write a story with this title:

'It was late and I was lost.'

Ask yourself questions:
Where were you?
When was it?
Who was with you?
Why were you there?
If you answer these questions, you will set the scene for your story.
Then ask yourself:
What happened?
If you give details of what happened, you will describe the events.

SOLUTION: Ideas for your story can come from your own life. Give yourself a minute to think if the title or the opening sentence describes something that has happened to you or a friend. It does not have to be very exciting.

SOLUTION: You have to be able to use past tenses well when writing a story, particularly the past simple and past continuous. Practise using these tenses by keeping a diary. Every evening write what happened during the day. For example:
I woke up this morning at about 7.00. I got out of bed and went into the bathroom. While I was having a shower, I heard my mother calling my name.

Keep it simple. Focus on forming the verb forms correctly and using the two tenses correctly.

SOLUTION: You will get extra marks if you show you can use adjectives and adverbs correctly. Remember: an adjective is used to describe a noun. An adverb gives information about a verb. For example:
There was a loud knock at the door and I got up quickly to see who it was.
Be careful: if you use too many adjectives and adverbs, your writing will seem unnatural.

LISTENING

Quick guide

What is it?

Paper 2: Listening tests how well you can understand conversations, talks and recorded messages.

Skills needed

In order to do well in the Listening paper, you must be able to:

understand main ideas and details.
- understand a speaker's opinion and attitude.
- answer questions within the given time.

Paper 2: Listening

The Listening paper has four parts.

Part 1 has seven short extracts from monologues (= a speech by one person) or dialogues (= speech by two people) such as conversations, recorded messages or radio programmes, and seven questions. For each question, you have to listen and choose the correct answer from three options, A, B or C. The options are pictures. (Total marks: 7)

Part 2 has a monologue or interview and six questions. You have to listen and choose the correct answer to a question from three options, A, B or C. (Total marks: 6)

Part 3 has a longer monologue. You have to listen and complete six gaps in a text. (Total marks: 6)

Part 4 has a dialogue and six statements. You have to listen and decide if the statements are true or false. (Total marks: 6)

Challenges and solutions

» **CHALLENGE 1: 'I don't know a lot of the words that I hear in the audio recordings or see in the questions.'**

SOLUTION: The instructions for the Listening paper are always the same. If you do the practice tests in this book, you will know what you have to do in the real exam. You will also hear each recording twice so if there is a word you do not understand the first time, listen for it again the second time.

SOLUTION: After the instructions for Parts 2, 3 and 4 there will be a pause to give you the chance to read the questions. This is very useful. By reading the questions first, you will start to get an idea about what the people will be talking about and you can guess what the answers might be. You will also have time to find the key words before you listen. Then when you listen, you will be able to listen for the right answers.

SOLUTION: Build your vocabulary. Start by downloading the *Cambridge English Qualifications B1 Preliminary* Vocabulary List from the Cambridge Assessment English website. This is a list of words that you should understand. Look through the list and make a note of the words you do not know. Then look up their meaning in a dictionary. Knowing these words will help you to do better in the test.

» **CHALLENGE 3: 'I find it difficult to decide if the statements in Part 4 are correct or incorrect.'**

SOLUTION: Part 4 is different from the other parts of the Listening paper because you have to understand a speaker's opinion or attitude. Learn the different expressions that speakers use to show they are giving an opinion, e.g. *I think...; In my opinion, ...; I feel ...* .

» **CHALLENGE 4: 'I don't always understand the speakers, especially in Part 4. Sometimes they talk too fast.**

SOLUTION: Listen as much as possible to natural English. The more you listen to native English speech, the better you will understand the English used in the *Cambridge English Qualifications B1 Preliminary* exam. Try the following:

• Watch TV programmes or films. The programmes do not have to be educational – comedies and dramas have good examples of natural spoken English. If you find this difficult, watch English-language films with subtitles. Listening can be easier when you can read to check understanding.

• Join an English language club. Your university, local library or community centre might have one. By joining, you will be able to practise speaking English and have the chance to hear native speakers.

• Join an online language community. There may be native speakers of English who want to learn your language and will be happy to practise talking to you using online tools like Skype™.

SOLUTION: Download English-language podcasts or radio programmes that you can store on your computer. At first, practise listening for only a minute or two at a time. As your comprehension gets better, listen for a longer time. When you listen, try and understand the speakers' pronunciation. Listen as many times as you need to until you understand the main ideas.

SPEAKING

Quick guide

What is it?

Paper 3: Speaking tests your ability to use spoken English.

Skills needed

In order to do well in the Speaking paper, you must be able to:
talk about everyday subjects and express your opinion.

- ask and answer questions during a conversation.
- speak clearly for about a minute.
- speak using a good range of B1-level vocabulary and grammatical structures.

Paper 3: Speaking

The Speaking paper has four parts.

In **Part 1** the examiner asks you some simple questions about your personal details, daily routine, past experiences, future plans, etc. (Time: 2–3 minutes)

In **Part 2** the examiner describes a situation and gives you and the other candidate instructions to talk about it. He/She also gives you a picture to help you. You have to make suggestions to the other candidate and reply to his/her suggestions, talk about different possibilities and agree about the situation. (Time: 2–3 minutes)

In **Part 3** the examiner asks each candidate to talk in turn. He/She gives you a colour photograph and asks you to describe it. You have to talk for a minute. He/She then gives the other candidate a different photo on the same theme. The other candidate also has to talk for a minute. (Time: 3 minutes)

In **Part 4** the examiner asks you and the other candidate to talk to each other about the theme of the Part 3 photographs and your own life and experiences. (Time: 3 minutes)

Challenges and solutions

» **CHALLENGE 1: 'I'm not sure how much I have to say when I answer the examiner's questions in Part 1.'**

SOLUTION: This part is just a simple conversation between you and the examiner. It is a chance for him/her to get to know more about you. You do not have to give very long answers but you should also say more than 'Yes' or 'No'.

SOLUTION: When you answer Part 1 questions, give a reason for your answer or an example. If the examiner asks *Do you enjoy studying English?* say why you do or do not enjoy it. For example:
Yes I do. I love listening to music and I am starting to understand the words to some of the songs.

If the examiner asks *What kind of food do you like to eat?* do not just reply *Indian food or Pizza.* Think of a meal you have eaten and why you enjoyed it. For example:
I enjoy Indian food. I often go to a restaurant near my house and I always order something spicy to eat.

» **CHALLENGE 2: 'I'm not sure I'll have anything to say in Parts 1 and 4.'**

SOLUTION: The questions in Part 1 and the conversation in Part 4 are about you and your experiences. The examiner might ask you to talk about your hobbies and interests, where you live, your family, your studies, etc. and you already know a lot about these subjects! Look at the table below. Think about the kind of questions the examiner might ask you about the subjects and how you would answer them.

Subject	Possible questions
Where you live	*Do many tourists visit your town?*
Your hobbies or interests	*Have you always had the same hobbies and interests?*
Your friends and family	*Who do you look like in your family?*
Your daily routine	*What time do you like getting up?*
Your studies	*What was/is your favourite subject at school?*
Your favourite TV programmes/films/books/music	*Have you read a book lately that you really enjoyed?*
The food you like/do not like	*What kind of food do people in your country like to eat?*

SOLUTION: Try not to repeat the same words and phrases all the time. For example, the following expressions all mean *I like or I don't like:*

- *I'm (not) fond of …*
- *I'm (not) keen on …*
- *I enjoy …*
- *I can't stand …*

In the same way, do not keep using *I think.* Sometimes use *In my opinion* or *I feel.*

SOLUTION: Remember that the Part 4 task is a conversation. You get marks for asking the other candidate questions and for responding to the things the other candidate says. This means you have to listen carefully because it will help you to keep the conversation going.

SOLUTION: Practise asking questions and using 'reply questions'. These are useful in a conversation. Here are some examples:

A: *I used to play football for my school.*

B: *Did you? Where you good?*

A: *I've never eaten Spanish food.*

B: *Haven't you? It's really nice.*

» **CHALLENGE 3: 'In Part 3 I worry that I won't have enough time to finish my talk or that I won't have enough to say.'**

SOLUTION: Time yourself when you practise for the Part 3 task so you get an idea what it feels like to talk for one minute. By timing yourself, you will learn not to speak too fast or too slowly and you will be able to give a complete answer within the time.

» **CHALLENGE 4: 'In Part 3 I'm worried that my description will be disorganised and I'll get into a mess.'**

SOLUTION: Practise using a structure for your description. Here is a suggestion:

- Begin by saying what the photograph is about. For example:
  This is a photograph of a birthday party. It looks like a children's birthday party.

- Talk about the people in the photograph and what they are doing. For example:
  There are lots of children and two adults. The children are sitting at a table and the adults are serving them food... (You could continue by describing what some of them are wearing or what they seem to be eating or doing.)

- Say what you think of the scene. For example:
  It's similar to the birthday parties I had when I was younger.

SOLUTION: There are many words and expressions that you can use to help you to organise your thoughts. In the table on the next page there are some common examples. Add new words and expressions as you learn them.

Use	Words and expressions
Comparing	*although* *but* *compared to* *However, ...* *On the one hand, ...* *On the other hand, ...*
Giving reasons	*because* *because of* *so* *in order to*
Giving examples	*for example* *for instance* *To give you an example, ...*
Adding	*The first reason is ...* *The second reason is ...* *Also, ...* *What's more, ...* *Finally, ...*
Concluding	*So, all in all ...* *To sum up, ...* *In general, ...*

» **CHALLENGE 5: 'I'm worried that the examiners won't understand me. My pronunciation is bad.'**

SOLUTION: At the beginning of Part 1, the examiner will ask you to spell your name. It is a good idea to begin well! Prepare for the exam by learning to pronounce each letter of the alphabet clearly.

SOLUTION: The examiner does not expect you to speak with the accent of a native speaker. In fact, having an accent is not a problem. The important thing is to speak clearly so that people can understand you.

SOLUTION: Ask your friends to listen to a recording of you speaking English. They might be able to tell you about pronunciation problems you don't notice on your own. In particular, ask them if it is easy to understand what you are saying. What words do they have difficulty understanding? Practise saying the words you had the most trouble with.

SOLUTION: Listen to as much English as possible. You could listen to English-language radio programmes while you work or watch English-language television in your free time. Start copying the sounds you hear.

SOLUTION: Practise speaking English with native English speakers. To find native English speakers in your area, try going to tourist attractions in your city. You could also join an English-language club at your school. If your school does not have one, check at your local library or start one yourself!

SOLUTION: Some speakers have trouble with certain sounds. For example, Spanish speakers sometimes add *e* to English words beginning with *s*, e.g. 'eschool'. Other speakers pronounce the letter *w* as a *v*. Find out if speakers from your country have a particular problem with English pronunciation and practise that area.

SOLUTION: If you want people to understand you when you speak, you have to stress words correctly. If you stress the wrong syllable, people might not understand you. For example, in the following nouns, the underlined syllable is stressed:

- *cele<u>bra</u>tion*
- *ad<u>ver</u>tisement*
- *phot<u>o</u>graphy*

However, in the verb form, a different syllable is stressed:

- *<u>cele</u>brate*
- *<u>ad</u>vertise*
- *<u>phot</u>ograph*

Knowing how to pronounce words with more than one syllable is important and you should use a good dictionary to check the stress of any new words.

» **CHALLENGE 6: 'I don't know what to do if I make a mistake and if I should correct myself.'**

SOLUTION: Correcting yourself when you make a mistake is a good way of showing the examiner that you do know the correct word or item of grammar. But remember: you must also show that you can speak for quite a long time and this will be difficult if you correct yourself all the time. It is probably best to correct some mistakes but try to relax and speak as fluently as possible.

SOLUTION: Practise speaking English as much as you can before the exam. One way to do this is to speak to yourself when you are alone. The advantage of being alone is that you will be relaxed and less worried about making mistakes. Talk about what has happened during the day, what your plans are for the rest of the week or your opinion of anything that is in the news.

Test 1

PAPER 1   READING AND WRITING TEST   (1 hour 30 minutes)

READING

Part 1

Questions 1–5

Look at the text for each question.
What does it say?
Choose the correct letter **A**, **B** or **C** on your answer sheet.

Example:

0

A The road has been repaired.

B The road will be open until Saturday.

C Use another road until Saturday.

Answer:

1

Hi Jane!
I'm at the doctor's and won't be back until about 4. Could you collect Mary from school? Call me if you can't make it.
Love, Mum x

Mum wants Jane

A to check that the doctor's appointment is at four o'clock.

B to phone if she can't get Mary from school.

C to phone the doctor's if there is a problem.

2

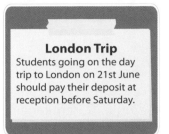

London Trip
Students going on the day trip to London on 21st June should pay their deposit at reception before Saturday.

A The total cost of the trip must be paid by Saturday.

B Meet at reception for the trip to London.

C Students will return from London on the 21st June.

3

Looking for a puppy?
A beautiful black and white puppy needs a good home.
Good with children.
Last one of seven so call Tom quickly if interested on **2291153**.

A Call Tom if you find a black and white puppy.

B The puppy would make a suitable family pet.

C You can choose from seven different puppies.

4

Product information!
Avoid contact with eyes.
In case of contact, wash eyes with clean water.
Can also cause skin problems. See a doctor if problem continues.

A Use eye protection when using this product.

B Wash your hands after use.

C Speak to a doctor if the problem does not go away.

5

To: jporter@homemail.com
From: peter@benziemail.com
Subject: Cinema

Hi Jake
Sorry, I can't make it to the cinema this weekend as a friend is coming to stay. Can we go next Saturday? Call me and I'll book the tickets.
Peter

What does Peter want?

A He wants to go to the cinema one week later.

B He wants his friend to get the tickets.

C He wants to bring another friend along to the cinema.

Part 2

Questions 6–10

The people below all want to start a language course.
On the opposite page there are advertisements for eight different language courses.
Decide which course would be the most suitable for the following people.
For questions **6-10**, choose the correct letter (**A-H**) on your answer sheet.

6

Sonia is going to Madrid for a business meeting and wants to practise advanced Spanish conversation. She works full time so she wants an evening class or one she can do at the weekend.

7

Tomas needs to pass his English exam to get into university and he is looking for a four-week full-time course. He isn't interested in social activities but needs accommodation.

8

Corinne, who is Spanish, starts university in the UK in the autumn and wants to improve her English. She is a little worried about attending lectures and has never written long essays in English.

9

Marie and her mother are going to Paris but don't speak French. They want to learn some basic expressions and would like to find out more about the French way of life before they leave.

10

Paolo and his wife Sandra want to take an English course for beginners and they like the idea of a school in the English countryside. They would also like to take part in social activities.

Language Schools

A Keele Business School

Business success means communicating with your customers. If you have relations with companies located in Spain, France or Germany, join one of our business communication courses designed to help you improve your advanced reading and writing skills. Contact us for more details.

B The Green Language Institute

Looking forward to a holiday in France? 'Get by in French' will teach you the language you need to make your holiday a wonderful experience. Learn how to ask for directions, order food and get help with health issues. The course also includes an introduction to the culture and customs of this wonderful country. Book a place now!

C Henley Language Academy

Our 'Academic Plus' programme is a three-month course to help you succeed in your university studies. Our full-time courses run from June to August. You will develop all the skills you need to survive in a university environment. Learn how to write lecture notes and essays, and practise your presentation skills.

D TTT Language Centre

If you are planning to go to university or need to show your level of English to an employer, the TTT Language Centre can help you. We know how important exam grades can be and our morning exam classes will prepare you for your chosen exam. In the afternoon you can socialise and enjoy visiting local places of interest on one of our weekly trips.

E Lake Language Centre

Learn English in the heart of the Lake District. Our small family-run school offers informal, morning lessons for all levels, with afternoons spent on gentle walks in beautiful countryside. Get to know other students and teachers even better in the evenings with our trips to top-class restaurants serving local specialities.

F Peak School

Peak School offers online lessons for people with busy lives. Join our one-to-one classes and learn or practise Spanish, French, German or Chinese with one of our highly experienced teachers. Simply arrange a time that suits you, log in to our online system and meet your teacher for your conversation lesson.

G Stonewell English

Stonewell English School offers language classes with a difference. Practise your English in the kitchen while learning how to cook delicious traditional English dishes. You will learn how to follow instructions in English and learn how to talk about food with the other students on the course.

H Blakemore School

Our full-time exam preparation courses start at the beginning of each month. Courses run for one to four weeks and will help you feel confident about your exams. If you want a taste of British culture, our family-run guest-houses offer a warm welcome. We also have one-bedroom apartments for students who prefer to live on their own.

Part 3

Questions 11–20

Look at the sentences below about information in a school newsletter.
Read the text on the opposite page and decide if each sentence is correct or incorrect.
If it is correct, choose **A** on your answer sheet.
If it is not correct, choose **B** on your answer sheet.

---

11 Mrs Sinclair will be working for fewer hours when she returns to work.

12 Parents have been complaining about the use of the Internet in school.

13 The e-Safety information sheets are for children to use when they do homework.

14 The e-Safety information sheets are not available yet.

15 All the children have attended an after-school club.

16 The school cannot promise that it will be able to offer classes in any activities parents ask for.

17 The school encourages parents to help with the after-school clubs.

18 The school needs more money to offer meals with better ingredients.

19 The school is not going to increase the price of school dinners immediately.

20 Parents with a low income can get help to pay for school dinners.

Highbury School Newsletter

Welcome to April's newsletter. There's a lot to tell you this month, starting with the news that Mrs Sinclair has given birth to a beautiful little girl. Mrs Sinclair would like to thank all the people who have sent her cards and wishes. We're looking forward to welcoming her back next term on a shorter, part-time contract.

E-Safety

Our teachers have been busy writing some excellent e-Safety information sheets for parents who are worried about keeping their children safe online. These sheets will give you some practical tips and suggestions to help you make sure your child is using the Internet safely. If you are interested, give your name to the school secretary and we'll contact you as soon as the sheets are available.

After-school clubs

Hopefully, your child has been attending one of our after-school clubs this year. With classes like 'Karate Kids' and 'Tiny Tennis', 'Children's Chess' and 'Kids Art', we've tried to offer something of interest to all our children. We've had several requests from parents whose children have not attended an after-school class for different activities. We'd like to point out that teachers run these clubs in their own time and the activities we offer depend upon their skills and knowledge. However, please keep giving us your suggestions; your ideas are welcome. And if you have any interesting skills and have a few free hours each week, please come in and talk to us.

School meals

We've managed to keep the price of school meals the same for the past two years. Unfortunately, because of the rising cost of ingredients, we'll be forced to charge a little more from next year. If your child has a meal only once or twice a week, the cost will be £2 per meal. For children having meals five days a week, the cost will be £9 per week. If you are unemployed or if you have difficulty paying for meals, please contact the school to see if financial help is available.

Part 4

Questions 21–25

Read the text and questions below.
For each question, choose the correct letter **A**, **B**, **C** or **D** on your answer sheet.

Career Choices

Dr Tom Halisham talks about life as a university professor.

I've worked at a university for many years. My opinion of university life when I started my first job was mixed. On the one hand, I enjoyed working in an academic environment and teaching a subject that I loved. But I also felt nervous about having so many very talented colleagues around me. They were experts in my subject and very well-known in the field of psychology.

However, I quickly got used to the job and over time I worked my way up to a senior position in the university. Being a professor is a very rewarding profession, mainly because the job involves so many different activities. I always go home at the end of the day feeling that that I've done something interesting. Some of my time is spent teaching classes or helping students with their research. I'm also expected to publish research of my own quite regularly, which can take up a lot of time. However, the reward is the chance to travel the world to share my research at conferences and to meet old friends and new colleagues. In many ways I'm free to decide what I want to research, which conferences I want to attend and, in some cases, what subjects I want to teach.

I once read that being a professor is regarded as one of the least stressful professions but things have changed over the years. Competition between universities has increased and as a result, what was once a relaxed, leisurely occupation is now much busier. Nevertheless, I think I'm very lucky to be in the profession I'm in. I'd certainly recommend it to anyone thinking of following a similar career.

---

21 What is Dr Halisham's main reason for writing this article?

   A to argue that being a professor has changed

   B to explain what his favourite activity is

   C to describe his job

   D to explain how he became a professor

22 Why does he like most about being a professor?

    A He earns a lot of money.

    B He can do different things.

    C He can spend time with his students.

    D He gets the chance to publish his research.

23 What do we learn about his research?

    A He does research into the tourist industry.

    B He wishes it didn't take up so much time.

    C He gets the opportunity to go to other countries.

    D He gets help from his students.

24 What is his attitude to being a professor now?

    A It isn't as enjoyable as it used to be.

    B There is more to do than before.

    C It isn't stressful any more.

    D He is in competition with his colleagues.

25 What would he write in his diary?

    A A busy week – but interesting.

    B I spent all week doing the same old things.

    C What a stressful week!

    D Another boring week comes to an end.

Part 5

Questions 26–35

Read the text below. What is the correct word for each space?
For each question, choose the correct letter **A**, **B**, **C** or **D** on your answer sheet.

Example:

0　　**A** most　　　　**B** very　　　　　**C** too　　　　　**D** much

Answer:

0	A	B	C	D
	■	□	□	□

The Nile crocodile

The Nile crocodile is one of the (**0**) .... frightening creatures in the (**26**) .... world. (**27**) .... the reptiles, it is second in size only to the salt water crocodile It can grow up to six metres in length and weighs up to 900 kilos. It lives in sub-Saharan Africa and is (**28**) .... in lakes and rivers.

It eats (**29**) .... anything. (**30**) .... fish make up most of its (**31**) ...., it also (**32**) .... any large animals that get too close to the edge of a river. This includes humans, hundreds of whom are said to be victims (**33**) .... year. Despite its reputation as a dangerous killer, the Nile crocodile is a good parent and, unlike many other reptiles, it (**34**) .... sure its eggs are protected (**35**) .... the minute they hatch.

26	**A** natural	**B** real	**C** normal	**D** wild
27	**A** Among	**B** Between	**C** With	**D** For
28	**A** discovered	**B** found	**C** met	**D** searched
29	**A** about	**B** most	**C** almost	**D** quite
30	**A** So	**B** Then	**C** Yet	**D** Although
31	**A** diet	**B** food	**C** meals	**D** menu
32	**A** fights	**B** battles	**C** attacks	**D** beats
33	**A** most	**B** the	**C** each	**D** all
34	**A** keeps	**B** holds	**C** takes	**D** makes
35	**A** up	**B** until	**C** along	**D** for

WRITING

Part 1

Questions 1–5

Here are some sentences about birthday parties.
For each question, complete the second sentence in each pair so that it has the same meaning as the first sentence.
Use no more than three words.
Write only the missing words on your answer sheet.
You may use this page for any rough work.

Example:

0   This year's party was not as good as last year's.

Last year's party was .... **this year's.**

Answer: | **0** | *better than* |

---

1   Sam was given money for his birthday by his parents.

Sam's parents .... **money for his birthday.**

2   Shall we have a party on your birthday?

Would you .... **have a party on your birthday?**

3   We can't invite everyone because our home is too small.

We can't invite everyone as our home isn't big ....

4   When everyone arrives, we'll sing Happy Birthday.

We won't sing Happy Birthday .... **everyone arrives.**

5   I always feel excited before I go to a party.

I always look .... **to a party.**

Part 2

Question 6

Your friend, Sarah, has invited you to a party to celebrate the end of her exams.

Write an email to Sarah. In your email you should

- wish her good luck with her exam results
- thank her for inviting you to the party
- ask if she wants you to bring anything to the party.

Write **35–45 words** on your answer sheet.

Part 3

Write an answer to **one** of the questions (**7** or **8**) in this part.
Write your answer in about **100 words** on your answer sheet.
Tick the box (Question 7 or Question 8) on your answer sheet to show which question you have answered.

Questions 7

- This is part of a letter you receive from an English friend, Carla.

> We are doing a project at school about breakfast around the world. Please tell me about breakfast in your country.
> What do you eat for breakfast? Do people eat different things?

- Now write a letter to Carla, answering her questions.

- Write your **letter** in about **100 words** on your answer sheet.

Questions 8

- Your English teacher has asked you to write a story.

- This is the title of your story:
  The knock at the door

- Write your **story** in about **100 words** on your answer sheet.

PAPER 2   LISTENING TEST   (approx 35 minutes)

Part 1

1 and 2

Questions 1–7

There are seven questions in this part.
For each question, there is a short recording and three pictures.
Choose the correct picture and tick (✓) the box below it.

Example: What did the boy buy from the supermarket?

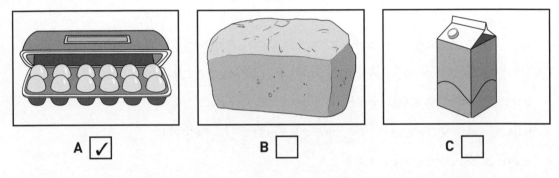

A ✓   B ☐   C ☐

---

1   Which place didn't the boy visit?

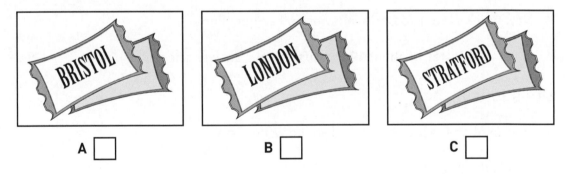

A ☐   B ☐   C ☐

2   What time does the film start?

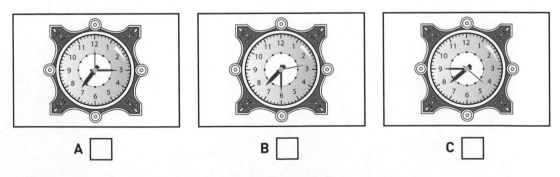

A ☐   B ☐   C ☐

3 What should the child take on the trip?

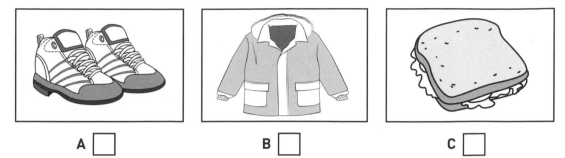

A ☐   B ☐   C ☐

4 What did the man do for the first time on his holiday?

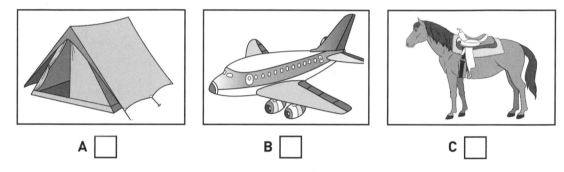

A ☐   B ☐   C ☐

5 Where did the woman last see her mobile phone?

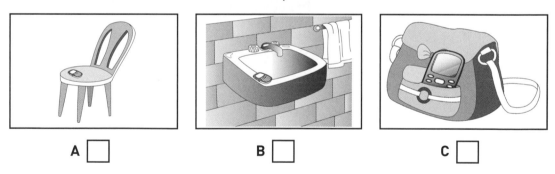

A ☐   B ☐   C ☐

6   Which item does the boy decide to sell?

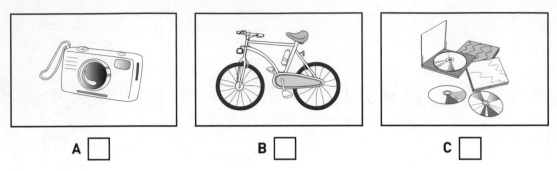

A ☐   B ☐   C ☐

7   How much does the chair cost?

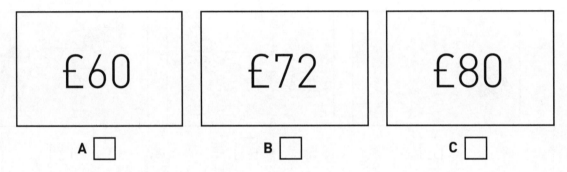

A ☐   B ☐   C ☐

Part 2

3

Questions 8–13

You will hear part of a radio interview with a man called Paul, who is talking about some of the jobs he did when he left school.
For each question, tick (✓) the correct box.

---

8 What was Paul's first job when he left school?

   A shop assistant ☐

   B waiter ☐

   C vet ☐

9 Paul thought his first job

   A didn't offer enough work. ☐

   B wasn't very interesting. ☐

   C didn't pay enough money. ☐

10 Paul's relative

   A gave him a job. ☐

   B knew he was unemployed. ☐

   C offered to help him. ☐

11 Paul thought

   A he didn't have enough experience to work at the animal rescue centre. ☐

   B the job at the animal rescue centre was perfect for him. ☐

   C the animal rescue centre didn't pay him enough. ☐

12 The job meant Paul had to

    A get up early. ☐

    B take some exams. ☐

    C go and live in a different place. ☐

13 In the last 20 years Paul has

    A been to Africa. ☐

    B been to university. ☐

    C changed his place of work. ☐

Part 3

4

Questions 14–19

You will hear a man talking about a photography course.
For each question, write the missing information in the numbered space.

Photography course

On some Tuesdays students visit local **(14)** ....

The tutor has been taking photographs for **(15)** .... years.

On Thursday students take photographs of **(16)** .... objects.

The course begins on the **(17)** .... July.

Full fees must be paid at the **(18)** .... of the course.

John is back in college on **(19)** ....

Part 4

Questions 20–25

Look at the six sentences for this part.
You will hear a woman called Hanna and her friend Joshua talking about doing long-distance running.
Decide if each sentence is correct or incorrect.
If it is correct, tick (✓) the box under **A** for **YES**. If it is not correct, tick (✓) the box under **B** for **NO**.

		A YES	B NO
20	Hanna is bored with going to the gym.	☐	☐
21	Joshua thinks Hanna isn't fit enough to do long-distance running.	☐	☐
22	Hanna plans to do as much running as possible before the race.	☐	☐
23	Joshua thinks long-distance running is easy.	☐	☐
24	Joshua understands that there are advantages to running compared to going a gym.	☐	☐
25	Hanna thinks she will enjoy preparing for the race.	☐	☐

PAPER 3   SPEAKING TEST   (10–12 minutes)

Candidates take the test in pairs.
There are two examiners. One of the examiners will talk to you. The other examiner
will listen to you. You will get marks from both examiners.

Part 1
This part of the Speaking test lasts for about two to three minutes.
There are two phases in this part:
Phase 1: One examiner will introduce himself/herself and the other examiner. He/She
will then ask you and the other candidate what your names are. He/She will probably
also ask you to spell them.
Phase 2: The examiner will then ask you a few basic questions. These may be about
yourself, your family, your home, your daily life, your interests, etc.

Part 2
This part of the Speaking test lasts for about two to three minutes.
The examiner will ask you to talk about something with the other candidate. He/She
will give you a drawing to help you. The drawing for Test 1 is on page i of the colour
supplement.
He/She will repeat the instructions before you start speaking.

Part 3
This part of the Speaking test lasts for about three minutes.
In this part, you and the other candidate will have a chance to talk by yourselves.
The examiner will give you a colour photograph to look at. He/She will ask you describe
it and talk about it.
When you have finished talking, the examiner will give the other candidate a different
colour photograph to look at and talk about.
The two photographs will have a common theme. The photographs for Test 1 are on
page ii of the colour supplement.

Part 4
This part of the Speaking test lasts for about three minutes.
The examiner will ask you and the other candidate to talk about the common theme of
the two photographs in Part 3. He/She may ask you to give your opinion or to talk about
something that has happened to you.

For examples of questions the examiner might ask you in the Speaking test, please go
to page 150.
For examples of answers that would get a good mark in the Speaking test, please go to
page 162.

PAPER 1   READING AND WRITING TEST   (1 hour 30 minutes)

READING

Part 1

Questions 1–5

Look at the text for each question.
What does it say?
Choose the correct letter **A**, **B** or **C** on your answer sheet.

Example:

0

A Call Sally to buy fruit or vegetables.

B The market needs a face painter.

C Sally is a children's face painter.

Answer:

1

A Mary will post the book to Sarah.

B Sarah can collect the book today.

C Steve will call Sarah.

2

A You must know the local area.

B You need to own a car.

C You can work in the daytime or the evening.

3

A There is no emergency service.

B The dentist is looking for new staff.

C The dentist will be open the next day as usual.

4

A The equipment costs extra.

B The owner can bring the bike to the customer.

C The bike is hard to ride.

5

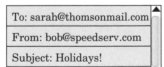

A Bob wants Sarah to come round once while he is on holiday.

B The plants should be all right without water until Bob gets back.

C Bob returns from his holiday on Saturday.

Part 2

Questions 6–10

The people below all want to go away for the weekend.
On the opposite page there are descriptions of eight weekend activities or holidays.
Decide which activity or holiday would be the most suitable for the following people.
For questions **6–10**, choose the correct letter (**A–H**) on your answer sheet.

6

Stephanie works very long hours during the week and wants to go somewhere quiet to relax. She doesn't want to have to cook and loves walking in the countryside.

7

Carlo would like to spend the weekend doing some voluntary work. However, he is recovering from a bad back so he can only do light physical work.

8

Susan and Terry would like to go away somewhere with their dog. They want to spend a couple of days near the seaside and be in walking distance of some shops and places of interest.

9

David is looking for a place with lots of museums, art galleries or theatres. He needs somewhere quiet to stay because he also wants to spend some time doing revision for an exam.

10

Mark and Sue want to spend their weekend learning a new skill. They would like a place that offers activities for their young children so that the whole family can have fun together.

Weekends Away

A Balmouth Weekend Breaks

Visit top galleries such as the SMART Gallery for the latest in the world of art. Or why not enjoy a night at one of the city's many theatres? Accommodation is in the city centre so you'll be able to enjoy the lively nightlife that's right on our doorstep, including our very own nightclub!

B Riverside Cottages

For anyone looking to get away for a quiet weekend in the heart of the countryside, Riverside Cottages are the perfect solution. Our short breaks include delicious home-cooked food, walks along some of the country's loveliest rivers and quiet evenings in our cosy cottages. No pets allowed.

C Dalton City Breaks

Sign up now for a weekend of culture. On Friday you'll enjoy an evening at the theatre – you can choose from three plays and a musical. Then on Saturday visit some of the world's great galleries before spending the evening in one of London's top restaurants. We have accommodation to suit every taste, from quiet guest houses to busy, city-centre hotels.

D Hertford House

Why not spend a few days helping out at one of the country's historic country houses? We welcome people of all ages and levels of fitness and can promise that you'll find something to enjoy, from working in our large gardens to welcoming visitors or helping motorists in the car park. Weekend accommodation provided at a generous discount.

E Westbury Gardens

If you have a weekend free and would like to join our team of gardeners, contact us for an enjoyable two days. We are busy returning the gardens to their former beauty. The work involves digging and carrying heavy equipment so you need to be fit. Because of the hard work involved, we cannot accept families with young children.

F Hollyoaks Guest House

Cheap weekend breaks at our 4-star guest house just five minutes from a quiet beach and in the heart of beautiful countryside. Ideal holiday for all the family. Pets welcome. A regular bus service will take you to the town centre eight kilometres way. This is well worth visiting for its great shops and activities for visitors.

G Hampton Farm

Come and join our farming family for a lovely weekend away from the busy city. Spend your mornings helping out with the animals and learn how to milk a cow. You can also join us in our in-house bakery, where you will learn how to make a delicious loaf of bread or pizza to take home with you. Great fun for all the family.

H Daisy Cottage

The autumn is a great time to take a weekend break in Weymouth, the seaside town with something for the whole family. Our lovely cottage is only minutes away from the busy shopping centre and tourist attractions. We also have a huge dog-friendly garden so your pet can have a great time, too!

Part 3

Questions 11–20

Look at the sentences below about accommodation for international students.
Read the text on the opposite page and decide if each sentence is correct or incorrect.
If it is correct, mark **A** on your answer sheet.
If it is not correct, mark **B** on your answer sheet.

---

11 Students are treated like members of the family.

12 Students give the rent money to the family.

13 Most students are likely to be 16 years old.

14 Families are expected to help students improve their English.

15 Students need only a bed and wardrobe for bedroom furniture.

16 Families sometimes take students with them when they go out.

17 One reason families take in students is to make some money.

18 It is not a good idea for young students to stay with older people.

19 Most families are very good hosts.

20 The school has never any problems with a host family.

Dear Student,

Thank you for your interest in living with a host family while you are studying at our school. Here are answers to some common questions students often ask.

What is a host family?
We find that many of our international students prefer accommodation with a local family. You can stay for as little as a week or for as long as a year. You are provided with a private room and your meals, and you live with your hosts as part of their family. We add the cost of accommodation to your course fees and we pay your host family directly.

Why do students choose a host family?
Some of our students are 16 years old and naturally, they and their parents want the security of family accommodation. Most students are also keen to learn about the British way of life and, of course, to have hosts who help them practise their English in a family setting.

What exactly does accommodation with a host family include?
Host families offer a good standard of accommodation. This includes a clean, nicely-decorated private bedroom. In addition to a comfortable bed and wardrobe, the room has a desk and chair for you to work at. Your hosts will spend time with you and include you in leisure time activities. This might be simply watching TV together or inviting you to join them when they make a trip somewhere.

Why do families act as hosts?
Of course, host families appreciate the extra money but they also have other reasons for acting as hosts. Older families enjoy the company of a young person, and younger host parents like their children to have contact with international students. Many of our families form lifelong friendships with their student guests and enjoy learning about their culture.

What if things go wrong?
In our experience, almost all of our host families have been extremely welcoming. Our accommodation office has a great deal of experience placing students with the right family and problems are rare. However, if there is anything you would like to discuss, you can contact our office at any time.

Part 4

Questions 21–25

Read the text and questions below.
For each question, choose the correct letter **A**, **B**, **C** or **D** on your answer sheet.

When I think back to the famous personalities of my teenage years, one name in particular comes to mind. Strangely, it isn't that of an American footballer, even though like other young people of my age I loved American football and had photos of my favourite players all over my bedroom wall. And believe it or not, it isn't the name of one of the many pop groups and stars my friends and I loved to listen to when we met to play our records. As well as these football and musical heroes, one person was very special.

Muhammad Ali, one of the most famous boxers of all time, was my biggest sporting hero. My family weren't boxing fans but despite this, we would sit around the TV to watch all of his big fights and would often laugh out loud when Ali was interviewed after the fight. For those younger readers who may not have heard of the great man, Ali was not only a great boxer, he was also a very entertaining speaker. He once famously described his style of boxing: 'Float like a butterfly, sting like a bee.'

He wasn't always popular. For example, I remember my father arguing with his friends about Ali's decision not to serve in the US army. However, my best memories were of the fights he had with another great boxer of the time, Joe Frasier. Many consider these fights to be the greatest of all time. I don't remember his early successes – his Olympic gold medal or the time when he beat World Heavyweight Champion Sonny Liston in 1964. But memories of his later career will stay with me for the rest of my life.

21 What is the writer trying to do in the text?

  A describe a personal hero

  B explain why boxing is such an important sport

  C discuss the life of Muhammad Ali

  D talk about his relationship with his father

22 What do we learn about the writer's teenage years?

    A There were various people he admired.

    B He wasn't like other teenagers.

    C He didn't have any other sporting heroes.

    D He used to play a musical instrument in a group with his friends.

23 The writer believes that Muhammad Ali

    A is as well known now as he was in the past.

    B attracted people who didn't normally watch boxing.

    C sometimes talked too much.

    D was never serious during interviews.

24 What does the writer say about Muhammad Ali?

    A He was wrong not to serve in the army.

    B He and Joe Frasier were the greatest boxers ever.

    C He was a better boxer when he was younger.

    D People sometimes disagreed about his actions.

25 What is the best title for this article?

A   **Family memories**   **B**   **A life-long hero**

C   **A man loved by all**   **D**   Boxing: the greatest sport of all?

Part 5

Questions 26–35

Read the text below. What is the correct word for each space?
For each question, mark the correct letter **A**, **B**, **C** or **D** on your answer sheet.

Example:

0   **A** none   **B** nothing   **C** little   **D** less

Answer:

0	A	B	C	D
	☐	▬	☐	☐

Growing tomatoes

There's (**0**) ...... like home-grown tomatoes. They taste
(**26**) ...... better than those you buy in a supermarket.
And as long (**27**) ...... you protect them from cold weather,
give them (**28**) ...... space they need to grow and (**29**) ......
sure they have the nutrients they need to be healthy,

you'll find a(n) (**30**) ...... plant can produce a surprising number of lovely tomatoes
for your kitchen. There are lots of different varieties so don't just grow the (**31**) ......
types. Small tomatoes have a sweetness (**32**) ...... children love, while the larger
ones are delicious in a salad or sandwich. The important thing to remember is to
(**33**) ...... the plants warm. Any (**34**) ...... of cold weather and you should cover the
plants or, (**35**) ...... better, grow them under glass in a greenhouse.

26	**A** so	**B** much	**C** lots of	**D** greatly
27	**A** as	**B** if	**C** though	**D** when
28	**A** much	**B** all	**C** more	**D** the
29	**A** take	**B** get	**C** make	**D** stay
30	**A** single	**B** one	**C** lonely	**D** only
31	**A** same	**B** like	**C** equal	**D** similar
32	**A** what	**B** that	**C** who	**D** where
33	**A** stay	**B** do	**C** keep	**D** make
34	**A** sight	**B** signal	**C** show	**D** sign
35	**A** even	**B** more	**C** still	**D** most

WRITING

Part 1

Questions 1–5

Here are some sentences about technology.
For each question, complete the second sentence in each pair so that it has the same meaning as the first sentence.
Use no more than three words.
Write only the missing words on your answer sheet.
You may use this page for any rough work.

Example:

0　　Shopping online is better than going to shopping centres.

　　　　I prefer .... online than to go to shopping centres.

Answer:　　| **0** | *to shop* |

1　　The laptop was heavier than I thought it would be.

　　　　The laptop .... light as I thought it would be.

2　　My friend said I should buy a new mobile phone.

　　　　My friend said, 'If I were you, ... buy a new mobile phone.'

3　　Starting the computer doesn't take long.

　　　　It doesn't take long .... the computer.

4　　This is the first time I have used this camera.

　　　　I .... this camera before.

5　　Shall I send you some of the photos I took on holiday?

　　　　Would .... me to send you some of the photos I took on holiday?

Part 2

Question 6

You have just started evening classes.

Write an email to your friend, Margaret. In your email you should

- tell Margaret what classes you are taking
- say where you are taking the classes
- explain why you are taking the classes.

Write **35–45 words** on your answer sheet.

Part 3

Write an answer to **one** of the questions (**7** or **8**) in this part.
Write your answer in about **100 words** on your answer sheet.
Tick the box (Question 7 or Question 8) on your answer sheet to show which question you have answered.

Question 7

- This is part of a letter you receive from an English friend, Mark.

> My parents are thinking of getting a pet.
> I know you have a dog and a cat. Which
> one do you think makes the best pet?
> Which one is easier to take care of?

- Now write a letter to Mark, answering his questions.

- Write your **letter** in about **100 words** on your answer sheet.

Question 8

- Your English teacher has asked you to write a story.

- This is the title of your story:
  The lights went out

- Write your **story** in about **100 words** on your answer sheet.

PAPER 2 LISTENING TEST (approx. 30 minutes)

Part 1

6 and 7

Questions 1–7

There are seven questions in this part.
For each question, there is a short recording and three pictures.
Choose the correct picture and tick (✔) the box below it.

Example: Which sport did the girl do at school?

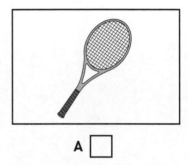  

A ☐   B ✔   C ☐

---

1 Which item of clothing does the man buy?

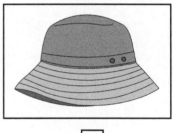  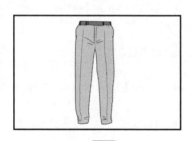

A ☐   B ☐   C ☐

2 What is the man going to have for lunch?

  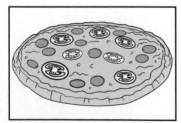

A ☐   B ☐   C ☐

3 What time will the woman be home from work?

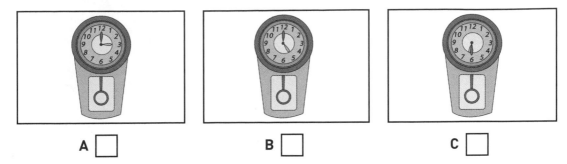

A ☐   B ☐   C ☐

4 How many people are attending the computer training day?

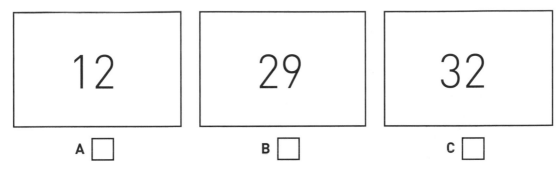

A ☐   B ☐   C ☐

5 What is the weather forecast for the day of the picnic?

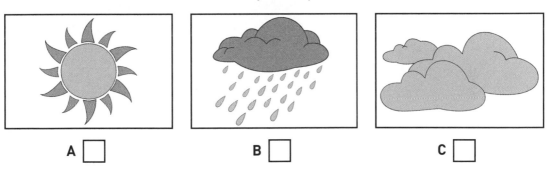

A ☐   B ☐   C ☐

6   Where is the woman's car?

A ☐   B ☐   C ☐

7   How did the man complain about his holiday?

A ☐   B ☐   C ☐

Part 2

Questions 8–13

You will hear part of a radio interview with a woman called Alice, who is talking about learning how to drive.
For each question, tick (✓) the correct box.

---

8 How old was Alice when she had her first lesson?

  A 17 ☐

  B 18 ☐

  C 19 ☐

9 Why didn't her father give her lessons?

  A He didn't have a car. ☐

  B He was worried that she would damage his car. ☐

  C Alice didn't want him to teach her. ☐

10 Alice found learning to drive

  A enjoyable. ☐

  B stressful. ☐

  C easy. ☐

11 On the day of her test, Alice

  A was ill. ☐

  B got up late. ☐

  C was nearly late for the test. ☐

12 At the end of the test

   A the examiner called his office. ☐

   B Alice spoke to her dad. ☐

   C Alice kissed the examiner. ☐

13 Alice doesn't have a car because

   A she doesn't need one. ☐

   B the car she wants is too expensive. ☐

   C she drives her father's car. ☐

Part 3

Questions 14–19

You will hear a recorded message with information about a children's dance class.
For each question, write the missing information in the numbered space.

Children's Dance Class

Do your children love dancing?

If the answer is 'yes', bring them along to our new classes, which are held every **(14)** ....

There are classes for younger children 5–10 years old and also older children 11– **(15)** .... years old.

Time: 3.30 to **(16)** .... p.m.

Classes start on 16th May and end on 11th July.

There will be a performance on 12th July. **(17)** .... will be available for £5 each.

There is no need to **(18)** ....

Call Melanie on 223 **(19)** .... if you have any questions.

Part 4

10

Questions 20–25

Look at the six sentences for this part.
You will hear a man called Mike and a woman called Carol talking about a film they have just seen.
Decide if each sentence is correct or incorrect.
If it is correct, tick (✓) the box under **A** for **YES**. If it is not correct, tick (✓) the box under **B** for **NO**.

		A YES	B NO
20	Carol has seen other films by the same director.	☐	☐
21	Mike liked the photography.	☐	☐
22	Mike wished he had read the book first.	☐	☐
23	Carol plans to get the film on DVD as soon as it is available.	☐	☐
24	Carol wants to go to the cinema again the following week.	☐	☐
25	Mike would like to see the same kind of film again.	☐	☐

PAPER 3   SPEAKING TEST   (10–12 minutes)

Candidates take the test in pairs.

There are two examiners. One of the examiners will talk to you. The other examiner will listen to you. You will get marks from both examiners.

Part 1

This part of the Speaking test lasts for about two to three minutes.

There are two phases in this part:

Phase 1: One examiner will introduce himself/herself and the other examiner. He/She will then ask you and the other candidate what your names are. He/She will probably also ask you to spell them.

Phase 2: The examiner will then ask you a few basic questions. These may be about yourself, your family, your home, your daily life, your interests, etc.

Part 2

This part of the Speaking test lasts for about two to three minutes.

The examiner will ask you to talk about something with the other candidate. He/She will give you a drawing to help you. The drawing for Test 2 is on page iii of the colour supplement.

He/She will repeat the instructions before you start speaking.

Part 3

This part of the Speaking test lasts for about three minutes.

In this part, you and the other candidate will have a chance to talk by yourselves.

The examiner will give you a colour photograph to look at. He/She will ask you describe it and talk about it.

When you have finished talking, the examiner will give the other candidate a different colour photograph to look at and talk about.

The two photographs will have a common theme. The photographs for Test 2 are on page iv of the colour supplement.

Part 4

This part of the Speaking test lasts for about three minutes.

The examiner will ask you and the other candidate to talk about the common theme of the two photographs in Part 3. He/She may ask you to give your opinion or to talk about something that has happened to you.

For examples of questions the examiner might ask you in the Speaking test, please go to page 153.

For examples of answers that would get a good mark in the Speaking test, please go to page 164.

Visual material for Paper 3: Speaking

Test 1, Part 2

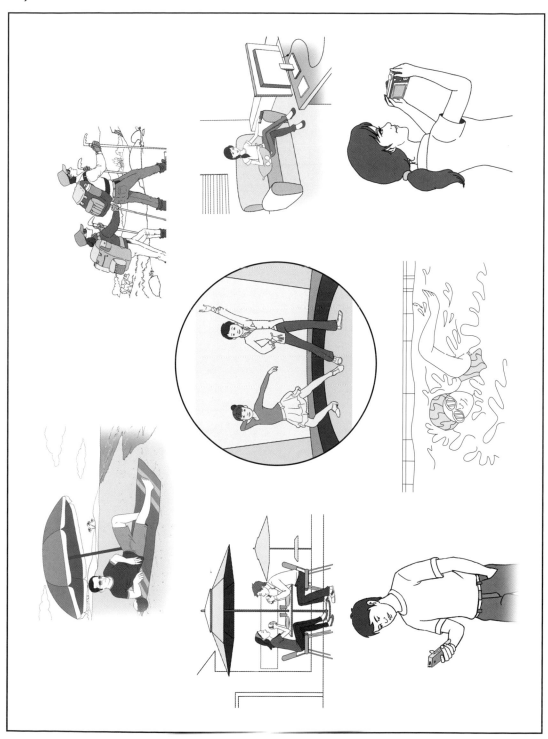

Test 2, Part 2

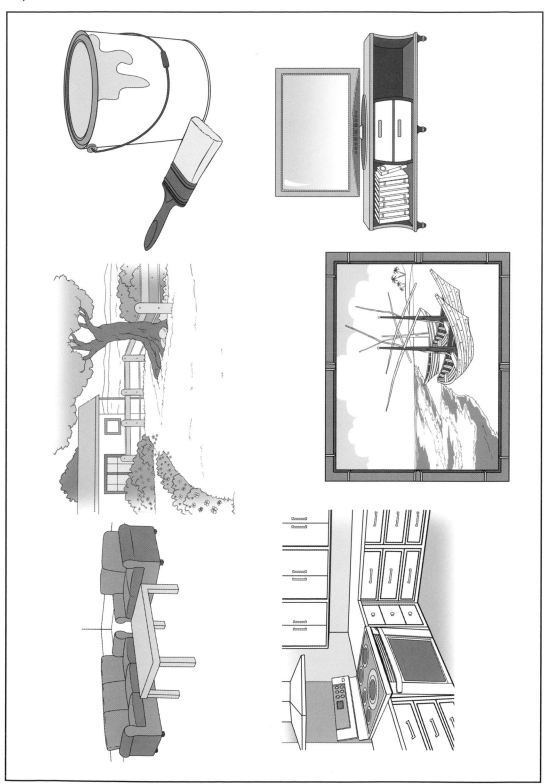

Test 3, Part 2

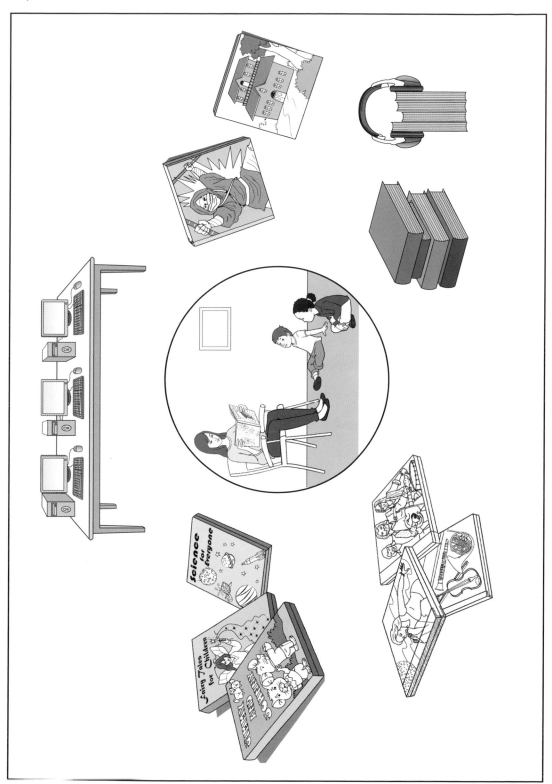

Test 4, Part 2

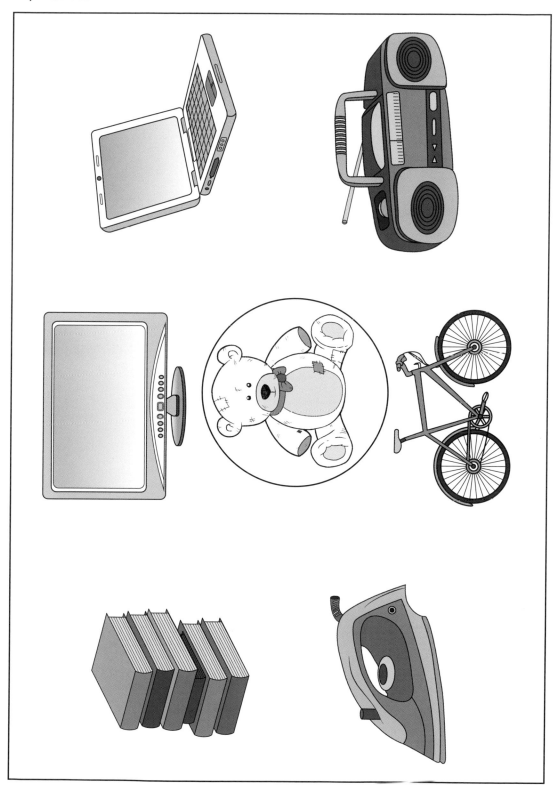

Test 3

PAPER 1   READING AND WRITING TEST   (1 hour 30 minutes)

READING

Part 1

Questions 1–5

Look at the text for each question.
What does it say?
Choose the correct letter **A**, **B** or **C** on your answer sheet.

Example:

0

Hi Stella,
I'm leaving for work now.
Sorry, but we've run out of
milk. There's a shop a bit
further along the road if
you need some. Help
yourself to breakfast.
Caroline xx

A   There's nothing to eat.

B   Caroline has gone shopping.

C   There's a shop near the house.

Answer:

1

We have moved!

This shop is no longer
open. We are moving to
34 Lewis Street.

Join us at our fantastic
re-opening next
Monday.

What is the news about the shop?

A   It is opening in a different place.

B   It is open until Monday.

C   It will not be at number 34 any more.

2

Mike, you left your bag in changing room. I took it to lost property office at gym. You can collect it any time. See you Saturday.
John

A John has Mike's bag.

B Mike can get the bag on Saturday.

C John can get his bag from the gym.

3

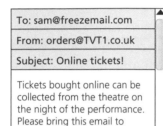

To: sam@freezemail.com

From: orders@TVT1.co.uk

Subject: Online tickets!

Tickets bought online can be collected from the theatre on the night of the performance. Please bring this email to prove you have paid.

A Tickets can be collected at any time.

B Customers must show they have paid for the tickets.

C Tickets can only be purchased online.

4

Need a gardener?

No job too big or small.

All rubbish taken away when the job is finished.

Call Tom for free advice.
87720937

A Tom needs a gardener.

B Tom does all kinds of gardening jobs.

C Tom does a lot of work for free.

5

Instructions

This product can be kept for up to 3 months before it is opened. Once opened, keep cool in a refrigerator and eat within 2 days.

This product

A will last for two days after it has been opened.

B stays fresh for three months after it has been opened.

C can be stored for three months before it is opened.

Part 2

Questions 6–10

The people below all want to go somewhere for a meal.
On the opposite page there are descriptions of eight restaurants or cafés.
Decide which restaurant or café would be the most suitable for the following people.
For questions **6-10**, choose the correct letter (**A-H**) on your answer sheet.

6

Nathan is at work and has forgotten to bring his sandwiches. He is a vegetarian, loves good coffee and wants to eat something he can bring back to the office for lunch.

7

Margaret is planning to surprise her friend and take her out for a spicy meal this Friday. She can't book a table because she isn't sure yet if her friend will be free.

8

Amanda and Alan have been married for three years and want to go out for a romantic meal on Sunday to celebrate their anniversary. They would like somewhere with music.

9

Ash is going out with his university friends to celebrate the end of exams. He wants a place where they can eat and then spend the rest of the evening dancing.

10

Vivienne needs to book a place for her daughter's ninth birthday party. She has invited twelve of her daughter's friends and needs a place that can provide both food and activities.

Eating out

A Michael's Nightclub

Every Friday and Saturday Michael's is the place to come for good food and lively, late night music and dancing. Enjoy a simple meal of fish and chips or something from our international menu. We're open till late.

B Sammy's

Only a few minutes' walk from the train station, Sammy's offers customers the very best in vegetarian cuisine. Don't forget to order your free tea or coffee with every meal. You don't need to make a reservation. Our doors open every evening at 19.30.

C Coolzone

Looking for somewhere special for your child's party? We're currently taking bookings for groups of up to 15 children. We serve a varied menu of favourites such as burger and chips, pizza or just plain sandwiches. Children also have the chance to enjoy our playground games and activities before and after their meal.

D The Moghul

The Moghul is one of the top Indian restaurants in town. We serve traditional, Indian cuisine in a modern environment. Our finely-spiced fish dishes are a particular favourite with customers. The Moghul is located in the centre of town and has a car park for customers. Call 0095538 to make a reservation.

E Placa de Piazza

Placa de Piazza is the place to go for couples who want to enjoy a special romantic evening for two. Start the evening with a delicious Italian meal and then enjoy a slow dance or two with your partner. We can promise you an evening to remember. Open 7 days a week.

F Nice 'n' Spicy

Enjoy spicy dishes from around the world at our self-service restaurant. Try one of our delicious Chinese or Thai dishes or, if you're feeling brave, one of our very hot Indian curries. Eat as much as you like for £15 per person. There is no need to book. We also have a non-spicy selection of meals for children.

G Ivy Cottage

The Ivy Cottage is the perfect place for a meal with friends or a romantic meal for two. It is also one of the town's most popular restaurants, and you will often find yourself sitting next to a well-known celebrity. We can promise you an international menu of top-quality food. Bookings must be made two months in advance.

H Natural Choice Café

The Natural Choice Café celebrates its tenth anniversary this year. We offer delicious vegetarian meals and tasty snacks, all made from fresh, locally-produced ingredients. We also serve teas and coffees from around the world. Eat in or take away. We are open from morning to early evening.

Part 3

Questions 11–20

Look at the sentences below about a lost dog.
Read the text on the opposite page and decide if each sentence is correct or incorrect.
If it is correct, choose **A** on your answer sheet.
If it is not correct, choose **B** on your answer sheet.

---

11 Tom Evans always used to let Sandy run free when he took her for walks.

12 Someone told Tom about Selborough Park.

13 At first Tom wasn't concerned when Sandy disappeared.

14 The park is completely surrounded by a wall.

15 Tom asked other people in the park to help him look for Sandy.

16 He then decided to go home and call the council.

17 Sandy was wearing identification.

18 The Evans family thought they would never see Sandy again.

19 Sandy was waiting at the door when Tom came home from work.

20 Tom doesn't plan to take Sandy to Selborough Park again.

Lost family pet returns

Two weeks after Sandy, the Evans' pet dog, ran off, her owners were shocked and delighted to discover she was still alive and well.

Sandy is a lively dog with lots of energy and every Sunday Tom Evans takes her for an extra-long walk. As Tom explains, 'She needs the opportunity to run free once in a while so I usually take her to an open space far from busy roads. I can't do that on her daily walk as there's too much traffic where we live. Two Sundays ago Sandy and I drove to Selborough Park, about ten kilometres away. A friend had recommended it as a good place for dogs.

'When we got to the park, Sandy spent the first half hour running around madly, as usual. She sometimes disappears for a moment or two but she frequently comes back to check I'm still there. So at first I wasn't too worried when she ran off and didn't return. My friend had told me there was a wall around three sides of the park and a river along the fourth side so dogs can't run away.'

However, twenty minutes later, Sandy still hadn't appeared and Tom started to feel worried. There were no other dog walkers in the park he could ask for help and even though he spent an hour looking for Sandy, there was no sign of her. Eventually, Tom called home and told his wife to ring the local council to inform them that the dog was lost. Sandy had a collar with her name and the Evans' phone number on it so there was a good chance that someone would find her. 'The drive back home was terrible,' said Tom. 'I knew the family were going to miss her and I was hoping she wouldn't get hit by a car or get injured in some way.'

Two weeks went by and the Evans family were now sure that Sandy would never return. Then, two days ago, Tom got a call from his eldest daughter as he was on his way home from work. She had returned from school to find a tired but healthy Sandy waiting at the door. 'Nobody knows how she managed to find her way home,' says Tom. 'I think we'll just use our local park from now on.'

Part 4

Questions 21–25

Read the text and questions below.
For each question, choose the correct letter **A**, **B**, **C** or **D** on your answer sheet.

The Internet affects the way we shop, how we communicate with each other, how we find answers to questions and much more. But for some time there have been concerns that the older generation are being left behind because they are unable to use a computer.

However, this is changing and several charities and community groups now help older people to get online. Paul Robinson runs one such charity, Seniors Online. Paul worked for an IT company before deciding to leave his well-paid job and start the charity. As he explains, 'I used to spend a few hours a week helping some older people use the Internet at the local library and I could see the difference it made to their lives. It can be quite lonely for the elderly when their children move away to find work and start a family of their own. Learning how to use email and receive photographs of their children and grandchildren was a wonderful experience for them. And when I saw what a big effect it had on their lives, I left my job and set up Seniors Online. We run training courses so that older people can enjoy the same opportunities as the rest of us.'

One of Paul's students is 89-year-old Betty, who had never used a computer in her life before she joined one of the classes. That was six months ago and Betty has now completed the course and received her 'graduation' certificate. 'I joined a class so I could learn how to use email to keep in touch with members of my family,' she says. 'That's been fantastic but the best thing of all has been learning how to research my family history online. Using a computer was a bit scary to begin with because you think you'll do something terrible if you press the wrong key. But you soon learn that you can't really break anything – and the teachers are very patient. I think all people my age should do a course like this.'

21 What is the writer trying to do in this text?

    A tell older people that they have to learn how to use the Internet

    B describe how the Internet can benefit older people

    C help Paul get money for his charity

    D encourage children to keep in touch with their elderly parents

22 Paul left his job with the IT company because

   A his salary there wasn't very good.

   B he realised how important the Internet was to older people.

   C he wanted to work in his local library.

   D he wanted to help parents find their children.

23 Betty started a computer course

   A to get a qualification.

   B to find out how to research her family history.

   C to learn how to send and receive emails.

   D to learn how to fix her computer.

24 According to Betty,

   A it doesn't matter if you damage the computer.

   B it can be difficult to use the keyboard .

   C the teachers take the time to help you.

   D you need to be patient to learn how to use a computer.

25 What might Paul say about the Internet?

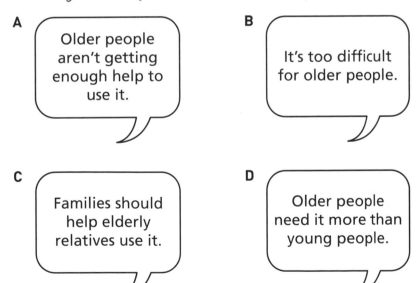

A Older people aren't getting enough help to use it.

B It's too difficult for older people.

C Families should help elderly relatives use it.

D Older people need it more than young people.

Part 5

Questions 26–35

Read the text below. What is the correct word for each space?
For each question, mark the correct letter **A**, **B**, **C** or **D** on your answer sheet.

Example:

0   **A** a   **B** the   **C** some   **D** any

Answer:

	A	B	C	D
0	▬	☐	☐	☐

Morris dancing

Morris dancing is **(0)** ...... kind of English dance that has
been around **(26)** ...... hundreds of years. There are many
different Morris groups around the UK. **(27)** ...... group
has its own style of dance that **(28)** ...... a story from the
area it comes from. Some groups dress up in plain white
shirts and trousers and wave a white handkerchief
around their heads. **(29)** ...... is claimed that this style of

dance dates back to a time **(30)** ...... the workers made fun of the rich landowners,
who used to follow the fashion of carrying white handkerchiefs. In another style of
dance you **(31)** ...... see groups wearing brightly-coloured clothes, decorated hats
and bells tied around their knees. The **(32)** ...... of the bells ringing is traditionally
meant to welcome the arrival **(33)** ...... spring. Morris groups sometimes include
musicians who play intruments. Morris dancers **(34)** ...... all over the UK and you
will find them at important festivals **(35)** ...... as on May Day or at Christmas.

26	**A** already	**B** for	**C** since	**D** in
27	**A** All	**B** Some	**C** The	**D** Each
28	**A** tells	**B** speaks	**C** says	**D** makes
29	**A** It	**B** They	**C** There	**D** What
30	**A** that	**B** who	**C** when	**D** which
31	**A** often	**B** normal	**C** usual	**D** frequent
32	**A** call	**B** sound	**C** noise	**D** song
33	**A** to	**B** at	**C** in	**D** of
34	**A** serve	**B** behave	**C** show	**D** perform
35	**A** like	**B** same	**C** such	**D** still

Part 1

Questions 1–5

Here are some sentences about travel.
For each question, complete the second sentence in each pair so that it has the same meaning as the first sentence.
Use no more than three words.
Write only the missing words on your answer sheet.
You may use this page for any rough work.

Example:

0   I have never been in a plane before.

      It .... the first time I have been in a plane.

Answer:

0	is

---

1   The journey was so long that I fell asleep on the train.

      It was .... long journey that I fell asleep on the train.

2   The bus stop is quite near my house.

      The bus stop isn't very .... my house.

3   I passed my driving test three years ago.

      It has been three years .... I passed my driving test.

4   You shouldn't take too much luggage on holiday.

      It's a good idea .... too much luggage on holiday.

5   I have never owned a car as fast as this one.

      This car is .... any other car I have owned.

Part 2

Question 6

You have just bought some books.
Write an email to your friend, Ellen. In your email you should

- tell Ellen what kind of books you have bought
- say where you bought the books
- explain why you bought them.

Write **35–45 words** on your answer sheet.

Part 3

Write an answer to **one** of the questions (**7** or **8**) in this part.
Write your answer in about **100 words** on your answer sheet.
Tick the box (Question 7 or Question 8) on your answer sheet to show which question
you have answered.

Question 7

- This is part of a letter you receive from an English friend, Cameron.

> We've just moved to an apartment near
> the city centre. It has lovely big windows
> and it's really close to the shops. What
> kind of place do you live in? Do you like it?

- Now write a letter to Cameron, answering his questions.

- Write your **letter** in about **100 words** on your answer sheet.

Question 8

- Your English teacher wants you to write a story.

- Your story must begin with this sentence:
  When the phone rang, I knew who it was.

- Write your **story** in about **100 words** on your answer sheet.

PAPER 2   LISTENING TEST   (approx. 30 minutes)

Part 1

11 and 12

Questions 1–7

There are seven questions in this part.
For each question, there is a short recording and three pictures.
Choose the correct picture and tick (✓) the box below it.

Example: What did the man do today?

A ☐   B ✓   C ☐

---

1   How is the woman travelling to the meeting?

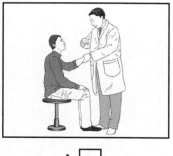  

A ☐   B ☐   C ☐

2   When is the builder going to do the work?

 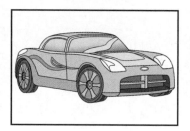 

Wednesday	**Thursday**	**Saturday**

A ☐   B ☐   C ☐

3   Where are the friends going to meet?

   **A** ☐

   **B** ☐

   **C** ☐

4   What is the boy going to wear?

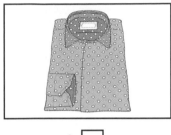   **A** ☐

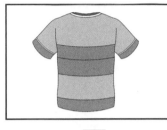   **B** ☐

   **C** ☐

5   How much does the camera in the shop cost?

£80	£95	£125
A ☐	**B** ☐	**C** ☐

6   Which present does the boy plan to give his friend?

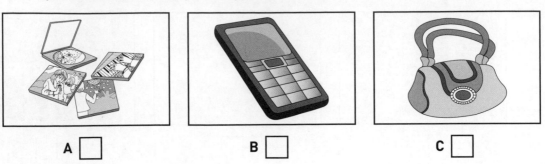

A ☐   B ☐   C ☐

7   What has the man broken?

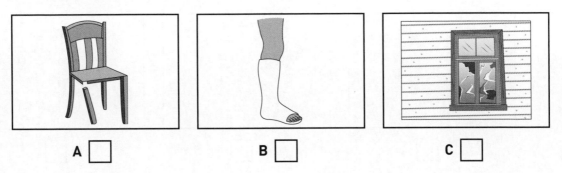

A ☐   B ☐   C ☐

Part 2

Questions 8–13

You will hear part of a radio interview with a woman called Mary, who is talking about a business she runs.
For each question, tick (✓) the correct box.

---

8 When did Mary first become interested in gardening?

    A as a child ☐

    B when she got married ☐

    C when she bought a house ☐

9 When did she decide to start her business?

    A after she lost her job ☐

    B after she read an article in a magazine ☐

    C after she spoke with a friend ☐

10 What caused her most problems at the beginning?

    A the weather ☐

    B customers' comments ☐

    C finding customers ☐

11 She gets most of new her customers

    A by advertising. ☐

    B from old customers who recommend her to others. ☐

    C by knocking on doors. ☐

12 If the work is very heavy,

  A her husband helps her. ☐

  B she pays someone to help her. ☐

  C the customer sometimes helps her. ☐

13 In the future she plans to

  A keep the business small. ☐

  B take on employees. ☐

  C go back to working in an office. ☐

Part 3

14

Questions 14–19

You will hear a radio presenter talking about an event in a nature park.
For each question, write the missing information in the numbered space.

Westwood Nature Park
Night Walk

Tour lasts 2 hours.

Café open for hot drinks and **(14)**..................

Please wear **(15)**.................. clothes.

Tickets available from the park **(16)**..................

Prices

Adult tickets: £10

Children's tickets: £5

Children below the age of **(17)**..................: free

Family tickets: £30

Next tour takes place on 15th **(18)**..................

Meet at park **(19)**.................. at 11.00 p.m.

Part 4

15

Questions 20–25

Look at the six sentences for this part.
You will hear a boy called Stewart and his friend Debbie talking about doing a class presentation.
Decide if each sentence is correct or incorrect.
If it is correct, tick (✓) the box under **A** for **YES**. If it is not correct, tick (✓) the box under **B** for **NO**.

	A YES	B NO
20 Stewart and Debbie are looking forward to the presentation.	☐	☐
21 Debbie thinks they have practised enough.	☐	☐
22 Stewart is worried that they might not speak for long enough.	☐	☐
23 Debbie has started looking for photographs.	☐	☐
24 Stewart reminds Debbie that they need time at the end of the presentation for questions.	☐	☐
25 Stewart and Debbie decide to meet the next day to practise.	☐	☐

PAPER 3   SPEAKING TEST   (10–12 minutes)

Candidates take the test in pairs.
There are two examiners. One of the examiners will talk to you. The other examiner
will listen to you. You will get marks from both examiners.

Part 1
This part of the Speaking test lasts for about two to three minutes.
There are two phases in this part:
Phase 1: One examiner will introduce himself/herself and the other examiner. He/She
will then ask you and the other candidate what your names are. He/She will probably
also ask you to spell them.
Phase 2: The examiner will then ask you a few basic questions. These may be about
yourself, your family, your home, your daily life, your interests, etc.

Part 2
This part of the Speaking test lasts for about two to three minutes.
The examiner will ask you to talk about something with the other candidate. He/She
will give you a drawing to help you. The drawing for Test 3 is on page v of the colour
supplement
He/She will repeat the instructions before you start speaking.

Part 3
This part of the Speaking test lasts for about three minutes.
In this part, you and the other candidate will have a chance to talk by yourselves.
The examiner will give you a colour photograph to look at. He/She will ask you describe
it and talk about it.
When you have finished talking, the examiner will give the other candidate a different
colour photograph to look at and talk about.
The two photographs will have a common theme. The photographs for Test 3 are on
page vi of the colour supplement.

Part 4
This part of the Speaking test lasts for about three minutes.
The examiner will ask you and the other candidate to talk about the common theme of
the two photographs in Part 3. He/She may ask you to give your opinion or to talk about
something that has happened to you.

For examples of questions the examiner might ask you in the Speaking test, please go
to page 156.
For examples of answers that would get a good mark in the Speaking test, please go to
page 166.

Test 4

PAPER 1   READING AND WRITING TEST   (1 hour 30 minutes)

READING

Part 1

Questions 1–5

Look at the text for each question.
What does it say?
Choose the correct letter **A**, **B** or **C** on your answer sheet.

Example:

0

This car park is for supermarket customers.

Cars can be parked for a maximum of one hour.

A Anyone can park for one hour.

B Customers can park their car for one hour.

C Customers can park for longer than other people.

Answer:

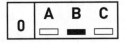

0	A	B	C
	▭	▬	▭

1

Did you enjoy the course?

Complete the form and tell us what you think. Forms should be left at reception.

A Collect your form at reception.

B There aren't any forms left.

C Use the form to give us your opinion.

2

> We tried to deliver a parcel but there was nobody at home.
>
> Please call Jane on 7724489 to arrange another delivery time.

A   Call Jane to agree on a new delivery time.

B   The parcel has been left at your home.

C   Jane wants to collect a parcel.

3

> Your phone bill for last month was £18. Money will be taken from your account on 3rd February.

The phone bill

A   was £18 for February.

B   was paid for last month.

C   will be paid on 3rd February.

4

> **Food served daily.**
> 9.00 a.m.–5.00 p.m.
>
> **Lunchtime Special Offer**
> 50% off all meals for the over 60s.

A   Meals are half price between the hours of nine and five.

B   There is special food for people who are 60 years old.

C   There is a lunchtime discount for people over the age of 60.

5

> To: colin@bakermail.com
> From: peter@limeserv.com
> Subject: Holiday
>
> Sorry about this but I need your deposit for the holiday. I have to pay the travel agent this week. Call me and let me know when we can meet.
> Peter

Peter wants Colin

A   to go to the travel agent.

B   to give him some money.

C   to book the holiday.

Part 2

Questions 6–10

The people below all want to buy something from a bookshop.
On the opposite page there are reviews of eight books and magazines.
Decide which book or magazine would be the most suitable for the following people.
For questions **6-10**, choose the correct letter (**A-H**) on your answer sheet.

6

Jessica is doing a project at school about classical music. She wants an introduction to the subject and would like to be able to listen to some examples.

7

Isabella is Spanish and has to give a talk to people in English. She would like to watch and listen to good English speakers making presentations.

8

Steve wants to encourage his daughter's interest in playing a musical instrument. She can play the piano quite well but would like to learn something different.

9

Roberto is Italian and is doing Business Studies. He needs information about a new exam and wants to see some example practice tests, especially for the Speaking paper.

10

Rebecca wants to start her own online business selling jewellery. She doesn't know much about computers and needs help to make a website.

Monthly book and magazine reviews

A 'Fully updated'

Preparing for the LLL Business English exam? *Skills for Business* is for anyone needing up-to-date practice in all four papers. This latest set of practice tests has been updated to cover the changes to the exam, including the Speaking tasks in Paper 4.

B 'Clear and practical'

This latest book from Hawthorn Publishers is aimed at those responsible for running websites for large businesses. It has clear, practical advice on how to make your company website easy to use for customers. It also includes hundreds of interesting ways to increase online sales through simple but effective changes to web design.

C 'Easy to follow'

If you believe playing an instrument is an essential skill, you'll have fun developing your abilities with this introduction to the guitar. Written in an easy-to-follow style, Teach Yourself the Guitar is suitable for all ages and will have you playing simple tunes quickly.

D 'Helpful advice'

In this month's magazine, read an interview with Sue Meyers, one of the examiners responsible for the changes to the LLL Business English exam. Sue will explain the reasons behind the changes and offer advice on how to help students prepare for the new tasks.

E 'Great tips and a free DVD'

Speaking to an audience is something that scares most of us, especially when English isn't our first language. Sound Great will give you all the help you need to speak with confidence. Follow the tips in the book and watch speakers putting these ideas into action on the free DVD that comes with it.

F 'A fascinating read'

Join thousands of music lovers who receive the latest news from the world of classical music. *Music Matters* is a monthly magazine written by musicians for musicians. As well as articles and reviews, it has interviews with composers, world-famous performers and young musicians just starting their careers.

G 'Clear explanations'

Tune In is a magazine for anyone new to the world of classical music. Each week an important work is presented: its structure is explained in simple terms and there is helpful advice on how to listen to it and what to listen for. The free CD will give you the chance to listen to the work as you read the comments in the magazine.

H 'Perfect for beginners'

Do you have a great idea and a clear market for your product or service? Technology can help you to keep your costs down and reach a global audience. *Go It Alone* is a new magazine that for people who would like to plan, design and publish their own website but who don't have advanced IT skills.

Part 3

Questions 11–20

Look at the sentences below about a UK festival.
Read the text on the opposite page and decide if each sentence is correct or incorrect.
If it is correct, choose **A** on your answer sheet.
If it is not correct, choose **B** on your answer sheet.

---

11 The 2012 London Olympics began with an event in the Cotswolds.

12 We do not know for sure when the Cotswolds Olimpicks started.

13 King James I was happy for the event to take place.

14 Robert Dover wanted rich people to give money to the poor.

15 Many of the sports people did at the Cotswold Olimpicks are known to us today.

16 Experts agree that Shakespeare wrote about the Cotswold Olimpicks.

17 During the seventeenth century everyone enjoyed the Cotswold Olimpicks.

18 People continued to hold the Cotswold Olimpicks during the English Civil War.

19 The British Olympic Committee support the Cotswold Olimpicks.

20 A member of the British royal family attends the Cotswold Olimpicks each year.

Cotswold Olimpicks

The 2012 London Olympic Games received the attention of the world but there has been another little-known Olympic event in the UK for hundreds of years. And it's an event which some say helped start the Olympic movement in this country. The Cotwolds Olimpicks take place every year on a Friday in spring. They are held in Chipping Campden, a village situated in a beautiful part of England known as the Cotswolds. It isn't clear when the first event took place but some claim it was as early as 1612.

The Cotwolds Olimpicks were the idea of a lawyer called Robert Dover but no one knows exactly why he organised the games. Some people say he wanted to encourage people to support their King and country. At the time England was ruled by James 1 and the king did indeed give the games royal approval. Another explanation is that Dover was keen to bring people together, in particular the rich and poor from the local community. Whatever the reason, the yearly games quickly became popular. People competed in familiar activities such as horse-racing, running, jumping, hammer throwing and wrestling; celebrities of the time attended it and poets wrote about the festivities. It is even claimed that Shakespeare mentioned the Cotswold Olimpicks in *The Merry Wives of Windsor,* though the play may have been written some time before the first games.

As the Cotswold Olimpicks grew in popularity, a group of people known as the Puritans started to object to them for religious reasons, saying they encouraged bad behaviour. The games came to an end at the start of the English Civil War but in 1660 they were re-introduced. Over time they became more and more popular and there are records of 30,000 people attending in one year. However, the games also attracted people who were more interested in the festivities than the sporting events. Eventually, they came to an end once again in 1852. However, this was not the end of the Cotswolds Olimpicks. They were re-introduced once again in 1966 and have since been recognised by the British Olympic Committee. Out of respect to their history, the modern games are watched over by a man dressed as Sir Robert Dover, riding on horseback and accompanied by a 'representative' of King James I. Unlike the real Olympic Games, the Cotswold Olimpicks last only about two hours and they are followed by celebrations in the village.

Part 4

Questions 21–25

Read the text and questions below.
For each question, choose the correct letter **A**, **B**, **C** or **D** on your answer sheet.

Life without the box

Could you live without a TV for one year? What would you do with all that spare time? Philippa Carling wanted to see if was possible and persuaded her family to give theirs up for one whole year.

'I live with my husband and our two children,' explains Philippa, 'and I realised just how much time we spent sitting in front of the TV. The children switched it on first thing in the morning and again when they got back from school. My husband and I were no better. We'd spend the evening together talking about very little other than what programme was on at the time. But then the family decided, after lots of arguments, that we would try to do without it for one year. We had the Internet and everyone was allowed to watch some of the recorded programmes if they had a good reason for doing so.' And so, on 24th July last year, the Carling family sold their TV.

Eleven months have now gone by and Philippa believes the experiment has been a great success. As she explains: 'We were all surprised at how easy it was. The immediate result was we all started to read a lot more, including the children. We spend time together after dinner playing board games around the table and the children finish their homework a lot quicker than before. We talk about what will happen when the year comes to an end and the children have always said they want the TV back. But they've also admitted that life has been good without it.'

So will the TV return when the year comes to an end next month? 'We're not sure,' says Philippa. 'We might decide to buy a new one or we might not. The important thing is we've all learnt that life can carry on without one. It can even be fun!'

21 What is the writer trying to do in this text?

    A explain how a family lived without a TV

    B persuade readers to give up their TV for a year

    C argue that TV programmes are boring

    D warn parents about the dangers of TV

22 What do we learn about Philippa's family?

    A She and her husband didn't watch much TV.

    B They argued about which programmes to watch.

    C They all agreed to try the experiment.

    D Their TV was on all day.

23 The family used the Internet

    A to watch TV programmes.

    B to find out which programmes they were missing.

    C to communicate with others who were doing the same experiment.

    D to find good reasons for not having a TV.

24 What does Philippa say about the experiment?

    A She was surprised at how much free time they had.

    B The children now read more than her and her husband.

    C The children's school work has improved.

    D It wasn't as difficult to live without TV as she had thought.

25 What might Philippa say about TV?

A

> It's best to watch TV when you have spare time.

B

> Life doesn't come to an end without a TV.

C

> Parents should stop children watching TV in the morning.

D

> Children find it too hard to live without TV.

Part 5

Questions 26–35

Read the text below. What is the correct word for each space?
For each question, choose the correct letter **A**, **B**, **C** or **D** on your answer sheet.

Example:

| 0 | **A** place | **B** position | **C** space | **D** piece |

Answer:

| 0 | A ▬ | B ☐ | C ☐ | D ☐ |

Death Valley

The hottest **(0)** ...... on earth is Death Valley, **(26)** ...... is located in the Mojave Desert in California. In 1913 the temperature there **(27)** ...... to an unbelievable 56.7°C. For many years the **(28)** ...... for the highest temperature had been held by the Mediterranean city of El Azizia **(29)** ...... northern Libya, where it was

thought the temperature was 58°C one day in 1922. However, in 2012 scientists decided that a mistake had been **(30)** ...... and that the temperature hadn't been quite this **(31)** .... Death Valley got its English name in 1849, **(32)** ...... people went there to **(33)** ...... for gold. The Native Americans called the valley 'tumpisa', meaning 'rock paint'. This refers to the paint that was made **(34)** ...... clay found in the area. Despite its name, only one person is ever known to have died in Death Valley **(35)** ...... the gold rush of the mid-nineteenth century.

26	**A** how	**B** where	**C** which	**D** what
27	**A** rose	**B** lifted	**C** came	**D** arrived
28	**A** goal	**B** score	**C** number	**D** record
29	**A** at	**B** in	**C** on	**D** with
30	**A** set	**B** made	**C** done	**D** had
31	**A** big	**B** strong	**C** tall	**D** high
32	**A** when	**B** where	**C** then	**D** since
33	**A** work	**B** find	**C** search	**D** go
34	**A** from	**B** by	**C** in	**D** for
35	**A** since	**B** during	**C** while	**D** when

WRITING

Part 1

Questions 1–5

Here are some sentences about exams.
For each question, complete the second sentence in each pair so that it has the same meaning as the first sentence.
Use no more than three words.
Write only the missing words on your answer sheet.
You may use this page for any rough work.

Example:

0   I suggest you do a practice test.

      You .... to do a practice test.

Answer:

0	*ought*

---

1   You should go to bed early the night before the exam.

      If I ...., I would go to bed early the night before the exam.

2   There are only a few questions on the exam paper.

      There aren't .... questions on the exam paper.

3   I registered for the exam four weeks ago.

      .... been four weeks since I registered for the exam.

4   I waited three months to get my exam results.

      I spent three months .... for my exam results.

5   Her father gave her a laptop for passing her exam.

      She .... a laptop by her father for passing her exam.

Part 2

Question 6

You won't be able to go to your friend Jane's birthday party because you have an exam the following day. Write an email to Jane. In your email you should

- thank her for the invitation
- explain why you can't go to the party
- ask her what she would like as a present.

Write **35–45 words** on your answer sheet.

Part 3

Write an answer to **one** of the questions (**7** or **8**) in this part.
Write your answer in about **100 words** on your answer sheet.
Tick the box (Question 7 or Question 8) on your answer sheet to show which question you have answered.

Questions 7

- This is part of a letter you receive from an English friend, Hugh.

> We're going on a camping holiday this year. Have you planned your holiday? What kind of holiday do you prefer?

- Now write a letter to Hugh, answering his questions.

- Write your **letter** in about **100 words** on your answer sheet.

Questions 8

- Your English teacher has asked you to write a story.

- This is the title of your story:

  A strange noise

- Write your **story** in about **100 words** on your answer sheet.

PAPER 2   LISTENING TEST   (approx. 30 minutes)

Part 1

16 and 17

Questions 1–7

There are seven questions in this part.
For each question, there is a short recording and three pictures.
Choose the correct picture and tick (✓) the box below it.

Example: When is the woman getting married?

June	October	November
A ☐	B ☐	C ✓

---

1   Which shop has just opened in town?

A ☐   B ☐   C ☐

2   Which fruit mustn't the boy eat?

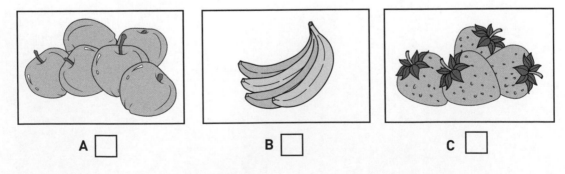

A ☐   B ☐   C ☐

3   What is the man doing on Friday?

A ☐   B ☐   C ☐

4   What kind of accommodation is the woman living in at the moment?

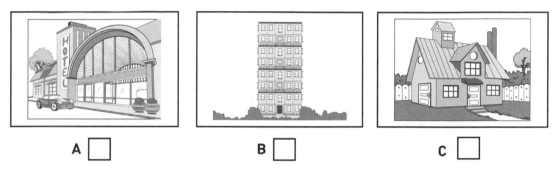

A ☐   B ☐   C ☐

5   Which item(s) is the man selling?

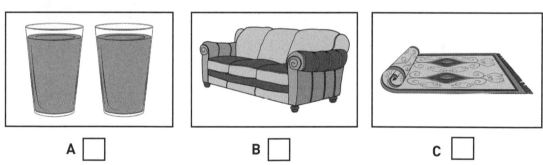

A ☐   B ☐   C ☐

6 How often does the boy see his grandfather?

Every day	Every week	Every month
A ☐	B ☐	C ☐

7 What has the woman forgotten to bring with her?

A ☐   B ☐   C ☐

Part 2

18

Questions 8–13

You will hear part of a radio interview with a woman called Fiona Josephs, who has written a book.
For each question, tick (✓) the correct box.

---

8 What do we discover about Beatrice?

   A She comes from a rich family. ☐

   B She used to live in Birmingham. ☐

   C She likes chocolate. ☐

9 The author decided to write the book because

   A Beatrice had an interesting life. ☐

   B Beatrice had started a school. ☐

   C she was interested in the Cadbury family. ☐

10 How does the author describe Beatrice's life when she was a child?

   A difficult ☐

   B unlucky ☐

   C comfortable ☐

11 What did Beatrice ask her brother to do?

   A stop giving her money ☐

   B let her meet the factory workers ☐

   C stop worrying about her children ☐

12 Why did Beatrice live in a tent?

  A She wanted her children to learn how poor people lived. ☐

  B There were too many people in her house. ☐

  C She wanted to live like poor people. ☐

13 What does the author say about Beatrice's children?

  A Some of them have read the book. ☐

  B The Cadbury workers offered them money. ☐

  C People who have read her book often feel sorry for them. ☐

Part 3

Questions 14–19

You will hear a radio announcement with information about a student film club. For each question, write the missing information in the numbered space.

University Film Club

The films shown include horror, science fiction, romance and **(14)** ....

The lecture theatre is located in the **(15)** .... Block.

Entrance to film nights on campus is **(16)** .... for members.

Every month there is a film **(17)** ....

There is a free end of year **(18)** .... in town.

Membership is only £10 per year. To join, contact Janet on **(19)** ....

Part 4

Questions 20–25

Look at the six sentences for this part.
You will hear a man called Don and his wife Angela talking about a family party.
Decide if each sentence is correct or incorrect.
If it is correct, tick (✓) the box under **A** for **YES**. If it is not correct, tick (✓) the box under **B** for **NO**.

		A YES	B NO
20	Don has bought the drinks.	☐	☐
21	Angela doesn't think they have bought enough food.	☐	☐
22	Angela wants Don to do the housework tomorrow.	☐	☐
23	Don is going to collect his mother from the station.	☐	☐
24	Don and Angela think the party will be a success.	☐	☐
25	Angela enjoys getting ready for family parties.	☐	☐

PAPER 3   SPEAKING TEST   (10–12 minutes)

Candidates take the test in pairs.
There are two examiners. One of the examiners will talk to you. The other examiner will listen to you. You will get marks from both examiners.

Part 1
This part of the Speaking test lasts for about two to three minutes.
There are two phases in this part:
Phase 1: One examiner will introduce himself/herself and the other examiner. He/She will then ask you and the other candidate what your names are. He/She will probably also ask you to spell them.
Phase 2: The examiner will then ask you a few basic questions. These may be about yourself, your family, your home, your daily life, your interests, etc.

Part 2
This part of the Speaking test lasts for about two to three minutes.
The examiner will ask you to talk about something with the other candidate. He/She will give you a drawing to help you. The drawing for Test 4 is on page vii of the colour supplement.
He/She will repeat the instructions before you start speaking.

Part 3
This part of the Speaking test lasts for about three minutes.
In this part, you and the other candidate will have a chance to talk by yourselves.
The examiner will give you a colour photograph to look at. He/She will ask you describe it and talk about it.
When you have finished talking, the examiner will give the other candidate a different colour photograph to look at and talk about.
The two photographs will have a common theme. The photographs for Test 4 are on page viii of the colour supplement.

Part 4
This part of the Speaking test lasts for about three minutes.
The examiner will ask you and the other candidate to talk about the common theme of the two photographs in Part 3. He/She may ask you to give your opinion or to talk about something that has happened to you.

For examples of questions the examiner might ask you in the Speaking test, please go to page 159.
For examples of answers that would get a good mark in the Speaking test, please go to page 168.

Mini-dictionary

 Here are some of the more difficult words from the practice tests. Definitions and examples are from *Collins COBUILD Essential English Dictionary.*

TEST 1: READING

cause /kɔːz/ (causes, causing, caused) VERB to make something happen • *Stress can cause headaches.*

encourage /ɪnˈkʌrɪdʒ/ (encourages, encouraging, encouraged) VERB to try to persuade someone to do something • *We want to encourage people to take more exercise.*

family-run /ˈfæmɪliˌrʌn/ ADJECTIVE controlled by a group of people who are related to each other • *a family-run hotel* • *small, family-run businesses*

force /fɔːs/ (forces, forcing, forced) VERB to make you do something even though you do not want to • *A back injury forced her to withdraw from the competition.*

hatch /hætʃ/ (hatches, hatching, hatched) VERB When an egg hatches, a baby bird, insect or other animal comes out. • *The eggs hatch after a week.*

highly /ˈhaɪli/ ADVERB used before some adjectives to mean 'very' • *Mr Singh was a highly successful salesman.*

income /ˈɪnkʌm/ (incomes) NOUN the money that a person earns or receives • *Many of the families here are on low incomes.*

manage /ˈmænɪdʒ/ (manages, managing, managed) VERB to succeed in doing something, especially something difficult • *Three girls managed to escape the fire.*

own /əʊn/ PHRASE If you do something **on your own,** you do it alone. • *He lives on his own.*

point out /pɔɪntˈaʊt/ (points, pointing, pointed) VERB to tell someone about a fact or show it to them • *He pointed out the errors in the book.*

repair /rɪˈpeə/ (repairs) NOUN something that you do to mend something that has been damaged • *Repairs were made to the roof.*

route /ruːt/ (routes) NOUN a way from one place to another • *Which is the most direct route to the centre of the town?*

socialise /ˈsəʊʃəˌlaɪz/ (socialises, socialising, socialised) also **socialize** VERB to meet other people socially, for example at parties • *I like socialising and making new friends.*

speciality /ˌspeʃiˈælɪti/ (specialities) NOUN a special food or product that is always very good in a particular place • *Paella is a speciality of the restaurant.*

succeed /səkˈsiːd/ (succeeds, succeeding, succeeded) VERB to get the result that you wanted • *We have already succeeded in starting our own company.* • *Do you think he will succeed?*

yet /jet/ ADVERB used when something has not happened up to the present time, although it probably will happen • *They haven't finished yet.* • *They haven't yet set a date for their wedding.*

TEST 1: WRITING

look forward to /lʊk'fɔːwədtuː/ **(looks, looking, looked)** VERB to want something to happen because you think you will enjoy it • *She's looking forward to her holiday in Hawaii.*

TEST 1: LISTENING

basin /'beɪsən/ **(basins)** NOUN a large bowl in the bathroom for washing your hands and face

career /kə'rɪə/ **(careers)** NOUN a job that you do for a long time, or the years of your life that you spend working • *She had a long career as a teacher.*

deal /diːl/ PHRASE A **great deal** of something is a lot of it. • *I've thought about this a great deal.*

fed up ADJECTIVE unhappy or bored [INFORMAL] • *My brother soon became fed up with city life.*

loaf /ləʊf/ **(loaves)** NOUN bread that has been shaped and baked in one piece • *He bought a loaf of bread and some cheese.*

qualification /ˌkwɒlɪfɪ'keɪʃən/ **(qualifications)** NOUN an examination result or a skill that you need to be able to do something • *I believe I have all the qualifications to be a good teacher.* • *All our workers have professional qualifications in engineering.*

rid /rɪd/ PHRASE When you **get rid of** something or someone that you do not want or like, you remove it. • *We had to get rid of our old car because it was too small.*

thrilled /θrɪld/ ADJECTIVE very happy and excited about something • *I was so thrilled to get a good mark for my maths exam.*

TEST 1: SPEAKING

bride /braɪd/ **(brides)** NOUN a woman on her wedding day, or a woman who is about to get married or has just got married

groom /gruːm/ **(grooms)** NOUN a man on the day of his wedding

reception /rɪ'sepʃən/ **(receptions)** NOUN a formal party that is given to welcome someone, or to celebrate a special event • *We were invited to their wedding reception.*

TEST 2: READING

argue /'ɑːgjuː/ **(argues, arguing, argued)** VERB to disagree with someone about something • *He was arguing with his wife about money.* • *They are arguing over details.*

cosy /'kəʊzi/ **(cosier, cosiest)** ADJECTIVE comfortable and warm • *Hotel guests can relax in the cosy lounge.*

despite /dɪ'spaɪt/ PREPOSITION used for introducing a fact that makes something surprising • *The barbecue was a success, despite the rain.*

dig /dɪg/ **(digs, digging, dug)** VERB to make a hole in the ground • *I took the shovel and started digging.* • *First, dig a large hole in the ground.*

even /'iːvən/ ADVERB used for making another word stronger • *Our car is big, but theirs is even bigger.*

former /'fɔːmə/ ADJECTIVE used for saying that a person or thing was something in the past, but is not that thing now • *There was an interview with the former president, Richard Nixon.*

hardly /'hɑːdli/ ADVERB used for saying that something is almost, or only just true • *I hardly know you.* • *I've hardly slept for three days.*

host /həʊst/ (hosts) NOUN a person or family who has someone staying at their house • *He was the perfect host for students at his home.* ADJECTIVE having someone staying at your house • *Living with a host family allows you to practise the language.*

keen /kiːn/ (keener, keenest) ADJECTIVE wanting to do something or very interested in something • *Charles was keen to show his family the photos.* • *Father was always a keen golfer.* • *I'm not keen on TV game shows.*

latest /'leɪtɪst/ NOUN **The latest** is the newest or most modern. • *Computers have always represented the latest in technology.*

likely /'laɪkli/ (likelier, likeliest) ADJECTIVE used for saying that a person or thing will probably do or be something • *These facts are more likely to be accurate.*

lively /'laɪvli/ (livelier, liveliest) ADJECTIVE, ADJECTIVE having lots of interesting and exciting things happening • *Torremolinos is a lively tourist town.*

long /lɒŋ/ **longer** /'lɒŋgə/ **longest** /'lɒŋgɪst/ ADJECTIVE lasting for a lot of time • *We had a long meeting.* • *She is planning a long holiday in Europe.* • *'How long is the film?'—'About two hours.'*

motorist /'məʊtərɪst/ (motorists) NOUN a person who drives a car • *Motorists should take extra care on the roads when it is raining.*

off /ɒf/ ADVERB away • *He was just about to drive off.*

skill /skɪl/ (skills) NOUN a job or an activity that needs special training and practice • *You're never too old to learn new skills.*

staff /stɑːf/ NOUN the people who work for an organisation • *The hospital staff were very good.* • *staff members*

sting /stɪŋ/ (stings, stinging, stung) VERB If an insect, a plant or an animal stings you, you feel a sharp pain when it touches your skin. • *She was stung by a bee.*

TEST 2: LISTENING

expect /ɪk'spekt/ (expects, expecting, expected) VERB to believe that something will happen • *He expects to lose his job.* • *We expect the price of bananas to rise.*

fill in /fɪl'ɪn/ (fills, filling, filled) VERB to write information in the spaces on a form • *When you have filled in the form, send it to your employer.*

traffic lights /'træfɪk ˌlaɪts/ PLURAL NOUN coloured lights that control the flow of traffic

way /weɪ/ (ways) PHRASE If you refer to doing something **the other way round**, you are talking about doing the opposite of what you have just said. • *It would have been better if we had done it the other way round.*

TEST 2: SPEAKING

fence /fens/ (fences) NOUN a wooden or metal wall around a piece of land

pour /pɔː/ (pours, pouring, poured) VERB to make a liquid or other substance flow out of a container • *She poured some water into a bowl.* • *She asked Tillie to pour her a cup of coffee.*

safety hat /'seɪfti ˌhæt/ **(safety hats)**
NOUN a hard hat that you wear to protect
your head

TEST 3: READING

advance /æd'vɑːns, -'væns/ NOUN **in
advance** before a particular date or
event • *We bought our tickets for the
show in advance.*

arrival /ə'raɪvəl/ **arrivals** UNCOUNTABLE
NOUN when a particular time comes
or a particular event happens • *He
celebrated the arrival of the New Year
with a party for his friends.*

booking /'bʊkɪŋ/ **(bookings)** NOUN the
arrangement that you make when you
arrange to have or use a hotel room,
theatre seat, table in a restaurant, etc.
• *The restaurant is now taking bookings
for Chinese New Year.*

claim /kleɪm/ **(claims, claiming,
claimed)** VERB to say that something
is true • *She claimed that she was not
responsible for the mistake.* • *The man
claimed to be very rich.*

concern /kən's3ːn/ **(concerns)** NOUN a
fact or situation that worries you
• *There were concerns about the safety
of the drug.*

fun /fʌn/ PHRASE If you **make fun of**
someone or something, you laugh at
them or make jokes about them.
• *Don't make fun of me.*

leave behind /liːvbɪ'haɪnd/ VERB If a
person, country, or organisation is **left
behind**, they do not achieve as much
as others or they do not progress as
quickly, so they are at a disadvantage.
• *I got left behind at school in maths.*

prove /pruːv/ **(proves, proving, proved)**
VERB to show that something is true
• *These results prove that we were right.*

purchase /'p3ːtʃɪs/ **(purchases,
purchasing, purchased)** VERB to buy
something [FORMAL] • *He purchased a
ticket for the concert.*

run away /rʌnə'weɪ/ **(runs, running, ran,
run)** VERB to leave a place because you
are unhappy or afraid there • *The girl
turned and ran away.*

run out /rʌn'aʊt/ **(runs, running, ran,
run)** VERB to have no more of something
left • *We ran out of milk this morning.*

store /stɔː/ **(stores, storing, stored)** VERB
to put things somewhere and leave
them there until they are needed
• *Store the biscuits in a tin.*

take away /teɪkə'weɪ/ **(takes, taking,
took, taken)** VERB to buy hot food in a
restaurant which you eat somewhere
else • *Do you want to eat in or take away?*

tie /taɪ/ **(ties, tying, tied)** VERB to fasten
or fix something, using string or a rope
• *He tied the dog to the fence.* • *She tied
her scarf over her head.*

touch /tʌtʃ/ PHRASE If you **keep in touch**
with someone, you write or speak to
them regularly. • *My brother and I keep
in touch by phone.*

up /ʌp/ PHRASE You use **up to** to say
how large a number is or how large
something can be. • *The rooms are
shared by up to eight people.*

TEST 3: LISTENING

coach /kəʊtʃ/ (coaches) NOUN a comfortable bus that travels between cities or takes people on long journeys

lift /lɪft/ (lifts) NOUN when you take someone somewhere in your car • *He often gave me a lift home.*

place /pleɪs/ PHRASE When something **takes place**, it happens in a controlled or organised way. • *The discussions took place in Paris.*

plenty /'plenti/ PHRASE If there is **plenty of** something, there is a large amount of it. • *Don't worry.* • *There's still plenty of time.* • *Most businesses face plenty of competition.*

remind /rɪ'maɪnd/ (reminds, reminding, reminded) VERB to say something that helps someone remember something • *Harry kept reminding me that we had to be there by 6 o'clock.*

seat /siːt/ (seats) NOUN something that you can sit on • *We had front-row seats at the concert.* • *The car has comfortable leather seats.*

smart /smɑːt/ (smarter, smartest) ADJECTIVE neat and right for a formal occasion or activity • *He looked very smart in his new uniform.* • *Members must wear a smart jacket and tie in the restaurant.*

spot /spɒt/ (spots) NOUN a small, round coloured area on a surface • *The leaves are yellow with orange spots.*

take on /teɪk'ɒn/ (takes, taking, took, taken) VERB to give someone a job • *The company has been taking on more staff.*

TEST 3: SPEAKING

tracksuit /'træksuːt/ (tracksuits) NOUN a loose, warm suit consisting of trousers and a top, that you wear mainly when exercising

TEST 4: READING

allow /ə'laʊ/ (allows, allowing, allowed) VERB If you are **allowed** to do or have something, you have permission to do or have it • *I'm not allowed to go to the party.*

approval /ə'pruːvəl/ NOUN when someone agrees to something • *The chairman gave his approval for an investigation.*

arrange /ə'reɪndʒ/ (arranges, arranging, arranged) VERB to make plans for an event to happen • *She arranged an appointment for Friday afternoon.* • *I've arranged to see him on Thursday.*

clay /kleɪ/ NOUN a type of earth that is soft when it is wet and hard when it is dry. Clay is used for making things such as pots and bricks • *a clay pot*

effective /ɪ'fektɪv/ ADJECTIVE producing the results that you want • *No drugs are effective against this disease.*

over /'əʊvə/ PREPOSITION more than a particular amount • *The house cost over £1 million.*

persuade /pə'sweɪd/ (persuades, persuading, persuaded) VERB to make someone do something by talking to them • *My husband persuaded me to come.*

reach /riːtʃ/ (reaches, reaching, reached) VERB to succeed in making people know about something • *Advertisers need to make sure they are reaching the right audience.*

rise /raɪz/ **(rises, rising, rose, risen)** VERB to increase • *His income rose by £5,000.*

search /sɜːtʃ/ **(searches, searching, searched)** VERB to look carefully for something or someone • *Police are already searching for the men.*

spare /speə/ ADJECTIVE not being used and therefore available to use • *I like playing computer games in my spare time.* • *They don't have much spare cash.*

term /tɜːm/ **terms** NOUN a word or expression • *Sodium chloride is the scientific term for table salt.* • *The leaflet explains everything in simple terms.*

update /ʌp'deɪt/ **(updates, updating, updated)** VERB to make something more modern or add new information to it • *We update our news reports regularly.*

TEST 4: LISTENING

crowded /'kraʊdɪd/ ADJECTIVE full of people • *He looked slowly around the small crowded room.* • *This is a crowded city of 2 million.*

rug /rʌg/ **(rugs)** NOUN a piece of thick cloth that you put on a small area of a floor • *There was a beautiful red rug on the floor.*

sorry /'sɒri/ **(sorrier, sorriest)** PHRASE If you **feel sorry for** someone, you feel sadness for them. • *I felt sorry for him because nobody listened to him.*

thriller /'θrɪlə/ **(thrillers)** NOUN an exciting book, film or play about a crime • *The book is a historical thriller.*

TEST 4: SPEAKING

embarrassed /ɪm'bærəst/ ADJECTIVE feeling shy, ashamed or guilty about something • *He looked a bit embarrassed when he noticed his mistake.*

Audio script

 **Track 01**

TEST 1   PAPER 2 LISTENING TEST

This is Cambridge English Qualifications B1 Preliminary, Test 1. There are four parts to this test. You will hear each part twice. Before you hear the recording for each part of the test, you will have time to look at the questions. There will also be time for you to check your answers. At the end of the test you will have six minutes to copy your answers onto the answer sheet. The recording will now be stopped. Please ask any questions now, because you are not allowed to speak during the test.

 **Track 02**

Part 1

Look at Part 1. There are seven questions in this part.
For each question, there is a short recording and three pictures.
Choose the correct picture and tick the box below it.
Here is an example:

What did the boy buy from the supermarket?

Mum:	Did you remember the shopping, Michael?
Michael:	Well, I've bought the eggs. Here you are, Mum.
Mum:	What about the loaf of bread?
Michael:	I didn't have enough money. If you give me some more, I'll go back and get it, and the milk as well.

The first picture is correct so there is a tick in box A.
Now look at the three pictures for question 1.

We are now ready to start. Listen carefully. You will hear each recording twice.

1 *Which place didn't the boy visit?*

Girl:	Have you seen this notice? There's a trip to London next week.
Boy:	Excellent! I went there once before.
Girl:	Yes, I'm looking forward to it. Did you go on the last trip? To Bristol?
Boy:	Yes. Don't you remember? We had dinner at that Italian restaurant. It was the trip to Stratford I missed. I had relatives staying with me at the time.

Now listen again.

2 *What time does the film start?*

Boy:	We're going to the cinema on Friday, aren't we?
Girl:	Yes, Friday evening. We're meeting at half past seven.
Boy:	But we'll miss the beginning of the film! It starts at a quarter past seven.

Girl: That's when the doors open. And there are always lots of adverts. We need to be sitting down by a quarter to eight when it begins.

Now listen again.

3 *What should the child take on the trip?*

Woman: Hello. This is Alison from the school. Just calling to let you know about the trip this week. There'll be a stop on the way for sandwiches but we'll make these at the school. When we arrive, we're going for a long walk. It might rain so your child will need walking shoes or boots. The centre provides raincoats so there's no need to pack those.

Now listen again.

4 *What did the man do for the first time on his holiday?*

Woman: So, how was your holiday?

Man: Great! Believe it or not, it was the first time I'd travelled by plane since I was a teenager. And I decided to go camping for a change, which was a totally new experience for me and I really enjoyed it. There was even a riding school next to the campsite so I was able to do some horse-riding.

Now listen again.

5 *Where did the woman last see her mobile phone?*

Man: Have you lost something?

Woman: My phone. It was in my handbag the last time I saw it.

Man: But I saw you take it out a minute ago. Then you put your bag on the chair and went off somewhere.

Woman: Oh, that's right! I took it with me into the bathroom and put it next to the basin. I hope it's still there.

Now listen again.

6 *Which item does the boy decide to sell?*

Boy: I need some money for a new laptop so I'm thinking of selling some of my things.

Mother: OK ... What about your CDs? You could sell some to your friends. Then there's your camera. You haven't used that for ages.

Boy: Mm ... I'd like to keep the CDs. Actually, I think I'll get rid of the camera.

Mother: Good idea, and you can let your brother have the bike. You don't use it very often.

Now listen again.

7 *How much does the chair cost?*

Woman: Excuse me, I'm interested in that chair – the one for eighty pounds.

Man: Actually, there's ten per cent off everything in the shop this week so the chair is seventy-two pounds.

Woman: That's nice, but I was hoping I could get it for sixty pounds.

Man: I'm afraid that's the cheapest we can let it go for, madam.

Now listen again.

This is the end of Part 1.

 **Track 03**

Part 2

Look at Part 2, questions 8–13.
You will hear part of a radio interview with a man called Paul, who is talking about some of the jobs he did when he left school.
For each question, tick the correct box.
You have 45 seconds to look at the questions for Part 2.

Now we are ready to start. Listen carefully. You will hear the recording twice.

Interviewer:	So, Paul, what did you do when you left school?
Paul:	Well, I'd always enjoyed being around animals and I wanted to be a vet but I never enjoyed studying at school and I left without any qualifications. I was interviewed for a job as a waiter but I wasn't successful. Fortunately, I had a friend who worked in a clothes shop and he got me a job there.
Interviewer:	How long did you do that job?
Paul:	About six months. It was a bit like school, really. I felt bored doing the same thing day after day and I worked long hours. But I loved having money to buy the things I couldn't afford when I was at school. In the end, though, I decided to leave.
Interviewer:	What did you do then?
Paul:	One day I met a relative I hadn't seen for a while. She worked in an animal rescue centre, where injured wild animals are given help and then returned to the wild. I told her I was looking for work and she offered to ask her boss if I could work for them. When they invited me for an interview, I was thrilled.
Interviewer:	And what happened?
Paul:	Well, during the interview, I made it clear it was the ideal job for me even though I had no experience. Anyway, I was offered a part-time job. The money was less than I'd earned in the shop but that didn't worry me.
Interviewer:	So what was the job like?
Paul:	It changed my life. It didn't feel like a job at all. I even enjoyed getting up early in the mornings. And it got me interested in education again. I started to think about getting qualifications so I could make a career out of it.
Interviewer:	And you *have* made a career out of working with animals.
Paul:	Yes. That was 20 years ago. Two or three years after I got the job, I thought about going out to Africa and getting experience of working with more dangerous animals. Then I read about a business course at university that looked interesting and did that instead. I'm still at the same centre – but now I'm the manager!

Now listen again.

This is the end of Part 2.

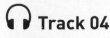 **Track 04**

Part 3

Look at Part 3, questions 14–19.
You will hear a man talking about a photography course.
For each question, write the missing information in the numbered space.
You have 20 seconds to look at Part 3.

We are now ready to start. Listen carefully. You will hear the recording twice.

Man: ... Good evening and many thanks for coming along. As promised, I'll now give you some details about our next photography course. Er ... We meet twice a week on Tuesdays and Thursdays in the Media Centre.

Our Tuesday evening class is spent examining photographs taken by local photographers and we'll take the opportunity to visit local galleries to see any exhibitions taking place. These visits are a great way to study the different ways experts approach their art.

Your tutor, Rob Waring, has been doing photography for 30 years and he'll be your guide. He'll explain what makes a good photograph and each week he'll focus on a different aspect of photography. He's a very popular tutor and I can promise you'll learn a great deal from him.

The Thursday session is more practical and will focus on taking photographs of simple objects. Together, the two sessions will give you a useful introduction to photography that will benefit anyone hoping to develop their skills.

So, if you're interested in signing up, the course runs for four weeks, with a starting date of 14th July. I suggest that you join quickly as there is usually a lot of demand and places get taken quite quickly. You don't want to be disappointed!

The cost of the course is £80 – that's £10 per session. You have to pay the full fees at the beginning of the course to guarantee a place.

So, if you're interested, please let me know as soon as possible. I'm on holiday for a few days and won't be in college until Monday so I suggest you see me then or soon after if you want to join the course.

Now listen again.

This is the end of Part 3.

 **Track 05**

Part 4

Look at Part 4, questions 20–25.
There are six sentences for this part. You will hear a man called Joshua and a woman called Hanna talking about doing long-distance running.
Decide if each sentence is correct or incorrect.
If it is correct, tick the box under A for YES. If it is not correct, tick the box under B for NO.

You have 20 seconds to look at the questions for Part 4.

We are now ready to start. Listen carefully. You will hear the recording twice.

Joshua: Hanna, you weren't at the gym today, well at least I didn't see you. I thought you always went on Friday?

Hanna: No, I wasn't there. In fact, I've decided I'm not going there any more. To be honest, I was getting a bit fed up with doing the same exercises all the time.

Joshua: But you can't just give up! Who am I going to talk to if you're not there?

Hanna: Well, why don't you join me in my next project? I was planning to ask you anyway. I've decided to try long-distance running.

Joshua: What?! Are you serious? You haven't done any running for years, have you?

Hanna: No, but I'm confident I can get fit enough if I take it step by step and don't try to do too much. There's a race in about seven months and I think I'll be good enough to enter if train. Why don't you join me? We can train together after work.

Joshua: I don't know. I've seen how hard that sort of thing is. I'm not sure I'd find it very easy.

Hanna: I know, but imagine how great you'd feel if you managed to run the whole distance. You can always start with short distances.

Joshua: True. And I suppose when you've completed one race, the idea of getting a better and better time makes you want to continue. The gym doesn't really do that, does it?

Hanna: I'm really looking forward to it, personally. It'll be completely different to the gym and I think it'll be a great way to keep fit – and good fun as well.

Joshua: OK, I'll do it! When shall I meet you for our first run?

Now listen again.

This is the end of Part 4. You now have six minutes to check your answers and copy them on to the answer sheet.

TEST 2   PAPER 2 LISTENING TEST

This is Cambridge English Qualifications B1 Preliminary, Test 2. There are four parts to this test. You will hear each part twice. Before you hear the recording for each part of the test, you will have time to look at the questions. There will also be time for you to check your answers. At the end of the test you will have six minutes to copy your answers onto the answer sheet. The recording will now be stopped. Please ask any questions now, because you are not allowed to speak during the test.

🎧 **Track 07**

Part 1

Look at Part one. There are seven questions in this part.
For each question, there is a short recording and three pictures.
Choose the correct picture and tick the box below it.
Here is an example:

Which sport did the girl do at school?

Father:	How was tennis? Did you win?
Girl:	We didn't play tennis today. The teacher was ill.
Father:	So didn't you do any sports?
Girl:	Well, we were going to play football but my friends and I decided to go running instead.

The first picture is correct so there is a tick in box B. Look at the three pictures for question 1 now.

We are now ready to start. Listen carefully. You will hear each recording twice.

1 *Which item of clothing does the man buy?*

Woman:	... Next, please. Would you like all these items, sir?
Man:	Well, I bought these trousers yesterday but they're too small. I'd like to return them.
Woman:	No problem, sir. As long as you have the receipt. And this shirt?
Man:	Yes. I'll take the shirt. Oh! And this hat was on the floor of the changing room. Someone must have left it there.

Now listen again.

2 *What is the man going to have for lunch?*

Woman:	Shall I meet you for lunch, James?
Man:	Good idea. We could try that new café in town. I've heard they make lovely sandwiches.
Woman:	I'd like a bowl of soup for lunch. I hope they have some.
Man:	I'm sure they do. And I'm going to have one of their pizzas. Well, see you at lunchtime.

Now listen again.

3 *What time will the woman be home from work?*

Woman: Hello, darling. I've got to work late this afternoon. I was hoping to leave by three o'clock but it looks like I might have to stay here a little later. The traffic will be worse then so I won't be back until around five o'clock. Don't forget my dad's coming round this evening. He said he'd be there at about six thirty. Bye!

Now listen again.

4 *How many people are attending the computer training day?*

Man: Do you know how many people are coming to the computer training day?

Woman: I think so, yes. There are 32 places and we're almost full now. I've just had a phone call from the IT department and they've asked us to take some of their employees. They've got 12 people who'd like to come. So if everyone comes, that'll be 29 people.

Now listen again.

5 *What is the weather forecast for the day of the picnic?*

Man: So, are you looking forward to the picnic on Saturday?

Woman: Yes, I am. According to the weatherman, it's going to be sunny.

Man: Huh! They said the same thing about last Saturday and it rained all day.

Woman: Oh, come on! It wasn't that bad. It was cloudy but it only rained for a little while.

Now listen again.

6 *Where is the woman's car?*

Paula: Hi Tony. It's Paula. My car's broken down.

Tony: Oh no! Where are you? Have you taken your car to a garage?

Paula: I'm waiting for a mechanic to come out and fix it. Can you believe it – I'm at some traffic lights and I'm causing a traffic jam!

Tony: Don't worry. I'll come and get you. I need to go to the bank anyway.

Now listen again.

7 *How did the man complain about his holiday?*

Man: ... Anyway, it was a terrible holiday and we're trying to get some of our money back.

Woman: You booked your holiday at the travel agent's, didn't you?

Man: Yes, that's right. I called them to complain but they never answer their phone. In the end, I filled in a form on their website. If they don't reply soon, I'll go and see them.

Woman: Well, I hope it's all right in the end.

Now listen again.

This is the end of Part 1.

Part 2

Look at Part 2, questions 8–13.
You will hear part of a radio interview with a woman called Alice, who is talking about learning how to drive.
For each question, tick the correct box.
You have 45 seconds to look at the questions for Part 2.

We are now ready to start. Listen carefully. You will hear the recording twice.

Interviewer:	Now, Alice tell me how you learned to drive.
Alice:	My school friends wanted to have lessons as soon as they were old enough and many of them started when they were 17. I decided to wait until my school exams were finished and to start lessons before I went to university at 19. But I was offered some money for a few lessons on my eighteenth birthday so I had my first one that same week.
Interviewer:	Does anybody else in your family drive?
Alice:	Yes, my mum and my dad both have a driving licence. But my mum didn't have her own car because my dad used to drive us everywhere. He often asked me if I wanted him to teach me but I didn't want to learn this way – I remember the arguments he and my mum had when he was teaching her! And I didn't want to have an accident and damage his car so I took lessons with a school.
Interviewer:	Did you enjoy learning to drive?
Alice:	It wasn't as bad as I'd thought it would be. My teacher was very patient. I expected to feel nervous and stressed on the busy roads but I actually found it exciting. That's doesn't mean it was easy. It took me a long time to learn some basic things.
Interviewer:	What happened on the day of your test?
Alice:	I'll never forget it! I got up early so as not to late. Then while I was getting ready, my little sister said she was feeling ill. My parents were at work so I had to find someone to take care of her before I could go out. I called my friend and luckily, she was able to help. But by this time it was getting late and I had to run to the test centre. I only just managed to get there on time.
Interviewer:	Did you pass?
Alice:	Yes, I did. The examiner was friendly but it was still unbelievable when he told me I'd passed. I could have kissed him! The first thing I did was to call my dad's office and tell him I'd passed.
Interviewer:	What kind of car do you drive?
Alice:	I don't have a car. My dad's offered me his because he's got a company car now. But I only have to travel to college and there's a good bus service where I live. Cars are expensive, so I've decided to wait for a while.

Now listen again.

This is the end of Part 2.

 **Track 09**

Part 3

Look at Part 3, questions 14–19.
You will hear a recorded message with information about a children's dance class.
For each question, write the missing information in the numbered space.
You have 20 seconds to look at Part 3.

We are now ready to start. Listen carefully. You will hear the recording twice.

Woman: Thank you for calling Sheldon Dance Studios. We are pleased to inform you that our dance classes for children are due to start soon.

As usual, the classes will take place every week. Unlike previous years, however, there will be two different age groups from this year. The junior class will be for children between the ages of five and ten, and the senior class will be for older children between the ages of eleven and fourteen.

We want to make it as easy as possible for children to attend – we realise that parents don't want to collect their children from school, go home and then leave again a short while later to bring them to their dance class. So we've decided to hold classes on Fridays, between half past three and half past four. This should give parents enough time to come straight to the dance studio from school.

Classes begin on 16th May and take place once a week, every week until the final class on 11th July. The children will take part in a public performance on 12th July to show off everything they've learnt on the course. The performance will be filmed and parents will be able to buy a copy of the DVD for £5. We're hoping to get as many people as possible to attend the performance so feel free to invite friends or relatives who would like to come along.

If you'd like your child to join one of the groups, just come along on the first Friday – there's no need to book.

And if you have any questions, call Melanie on 223 1457.

Now listen again.

This is the end of Part 3.

 Track 10

Part 4

Look at Part 4, questions 20–25.
There are six sentences for this part.
You will hear a conversation between a man, Mike, and a woman, Carol who are talking about a film they have just seen.
Decide if each sentence is correct or incorrect.
If it is correct, tick the box under A for YES. If it is not correct, tick the box under B for NO.
You have 20 seconds to look at the questions for Part 4.

We are now ready to start. Listen carefully. You will hear the recording twice.

Mike: Well, that was a long film, wasn't it? I was getting a little bored towards the end.

Carol: That's typical of that director's films. They're all long. So I've been told, anyway. That's the only one I've seen.

Mike: I can't say I really enjoyed it, to be honest. The photography was amazing but I found it difficult to follow the story. It didn't really make much sense to me.

Carol: Yes, I think the story can be a little confusing if you haven't read the book first. You haven't read it, have you?

Mike: I bought it the other week but decided to read it after I'd seen the film. If only I'd done things the other way round! I might have understood what was going on.

Carol: I hear we can buy it on DVD soon. Why don't you get it when it's in the shops? We could both watch it again to see if it's better the second time.

Mike: Yes, that's a good idea. I'll let you know when I've bought a copy. So, shall we get together again soon?

Carol: What about the same time next week? They're showing that film we were talking about the other day, that police thriller. Remember?

Mike: Yes. That'll be nice. I'll get the tickets this time as you paid this evening. And a thriller, yes. It'll be good to see something different next week.

Carol: OK. See you next week then.

Now listen again.

This is the end of Part 4. You now have six minutes to check your answers and copy them on to the answer sheet.

 **Track 11**

TEST 3   PAPER 2 LISTENING TEST

This is Cambridge English Qualifications B1 Preliminary, Test 3. There are four parts to this test. You will hear each part twice. Before you hear the recording for each part of the test, you will have time to look at the questions. There will also be time for you to check your answers. At the end of the test you will have six minutes to copy your answers onto the answer sheet. The recording will now be stopped. Please ask any questions now, because you are not allowed to speak during the test.

 **Track 12**
Part 1

Look at Part one. There are seven questions in this part.
For each question, there is a short recording and three pictures.
Choose the correct picture and tick the box below it.
Here is an example:

What did the man do today?

Woman:	Hello, Bob. How are you feeling today?
Man:	Oh, not bad. I've got a bit of a cough but it isn't serious so I didn't bother to go to the doctor.
Woman:	I suppose you've been working on your car again.
Man:	Actually, no. It was such a nice day that I went for a walk in the park.

The second picture is correct so there is a tick in box B. Now look at the pictures for question 1.

We are now ready to start. Listen carefully. You will hear each recording twice.

1 *How is the woman travelling to the meeting?*

Man:	So, are you ready for your meeting?
Woman:	Yes, I think so. I was planning to go by coach but there isn't one today. There's a train at nine thirty, though, so I'm going to catch that.
Man:	I'll get the car out of the garage and give you a lift to the station.
Woman:	Oh, that would be great. Thanks.

Now listen again.

2 *When is the builder going to do the work?*

Builder:	... So if that's everything, I'll order the materials.
Woman:	Great. When will you be able to do the job? I've got visitors on Saturday and I'd like to have everything finished before then. Could you come on Wednesday?
Builder:	Yes, I can do Wednesday but I might not have the materials by then. What about the next day, Thursday? I can be here early in the morning.
Woman:	OK. I'll see you then.

Now listen again.

3 *Where are the friends going to meet?*

Linda:	Hi Carol. I'm just calling about our theatre night on Friday. I've spoken to everyone else and we've decided to meet about an hour before the play starts. I've booked the seats, by the way – we're right at the front. And there's a car park at the back of the theatre if you're going to drive. We'll be in the café across the road waiting for you. I'll order you a coffee.

Now listen again.

4 *What is the boy going to wear?*

Mother:	Steven! You can't wear that T-shirt!
Boy:	Why not? You've already told me I can't wear the shirt with the spots. What's wrong with this T-shirt?
Mother:	It's not smart enough for a wedding. Now take it off and put on the nice jumper I bought for you.
Boy:	Oh, all right. I'll wear it – but I don't like it.

Now listen again.

5 *How much does the camera in the shop cost?*

Woman:	Could I have a look at the camera on the shelf?
Shop assistant:	Here you are, madam. It's the latest model.

| Woman: | I've seen it advertised online for £80. What are you selling it for? |
| Shop assistant: | £80 seems very cheap to me. We're currently selling it for £95 – it usually sells for £125 but we have a special offer at the moment. |

Now listen again.

6 *Which present does the boy plan to give his friend?*

Girl:	Have you bought Sarah's present yet? It's her birthday on Saturday.
Boy:	Yes, I know. I'd love to buy her that phone she likes but I don't have much money.
Girl:	Well, what about that handbag she was looking at in the shop?
Boy:	Actually, I'm getting her a couple of CDs. She bought the handbag herself yesterday.

Now listen again.

7 *What has the man broken?*

| Man: | Hello, it's me. I'm just on my way to get Billy from school. If you get home before me, you'll see I had a little accident while you were out. I was standing on the chair to clean the windows and one of the legs broke. I'm perfectly OK and I'm sure we can get it fixed. I'll ask a few friends if they know anyone who can do it. |

Now listen again.

This is the end of Part 1.

 Track 13
Part 2

Look at Part 2, questions 8–13.
You will hear part of a radio interview with a woman called Mary, who is talking about her gardening business.
For each question, tick the correct box.
You have 45 seconds to look at the questions for Part 2.

We are now ready to start. Listen carefully. You will hear the recording twice.

Interviewer:	... And in the studio today is Mary Williams, who's going to speak to us about her gardening business. Mary, have you always been fond of gardening?
Mary:	Not at all, no. My parents had a lovely garden but like most children, I just wasn't interested. And when I got married, we lived in an apartment so gardening wasn't possible. Then a few years ago my husband and I moved into a house and I decided I was going to make the garden beautiful.
Interviewer:	So how did a hobby become a business?
Mary:	Well, I read an article about a woman who'd lost her job. She used her savings to start her own business. That made me think. My friends often told me I was a good gardener – and I thought: Why not?
Interviewer:	How did you get started?

Mary:	Oh ... doing small jobs for friends and relatives and I soon found myself getting plenty of work. But there was a lot of rain during that first year, so some jobs took longer than planned. But I got nice comments from people when the jobs *were* finished.
Interviewer:	And how are you getting on now?
Mary:	Very well. I get a lot of new customers from people who have recommended me and I haven't needed to look for work by knocking on doors – not yet, anyway. I do advertise, but that's just a few notices in shop windows.
Interviewer:	Do you do all the work on your own?
Mary:	Most of the time, yes. Sometimes customers help me so they can keep costs down. And sometimes women get their husbands to do some of the digging or heavy lifting. I occasionally pay a friend to deliver things from the garden centre – but that's all.
Interviewer:	So where do you see the business in five years' time?
Mary:	I don't want to take on more jobs than I can do myself. If I did that, I'd have to employ people, which I don't want to do. And I certainly have no plans to go back to working in an office.

Now listen again.

This is the end of Part 2.

 **Track 14**

Part 3

Look at Part 3, questions 14–19.
You will hear a radio presenter talking about an event in a nature park.
For each question, write the missing information in the numbered space.
You have 20 seconds to look at Part 3.

We are now ready to start. Listen carefully. You will hear the recording twice.

Woman:	And now some information about an interesting event that will be taking place in the area this month. Westwood Nature Park is organising another of its 'night walks'. These walks are extremely popular and the available places are booked very quickly.
	As usual, the park's team of naturalists will be taking members of the public on a guided tour to see the wild creatures that come out after it gets dark. The team are all experts and will be able to answer any questions you might have. The walk lasts about two hours and ends with a cup of hot soup and the chance to meet others around a camp fire. And don't worry. If you can't wait for the soup or if you're very hungry, the park café will be open till late, serving tea, coffee and snacks. The temperature is likely to drop at that time of night so please remember to put on warm clothes. Families are welcome to join the walk. If you do bring young children, though, please remember to keep them with you at all times.

If you'd like to join the next walk, you can buy tickets from the park website from this Friday. Adult tickets cost £10 each and children's tickets are £5. If you have children younger than six, they can join the walk for free. They are also selling family tickets that allow entry for up to five people. These cost £30.

The next tour takes place on 15th July. Once you've bought your tickets, you'll be invited to join the group at the park entrance at 11.00 p.m.

Now listen again.

This is the end of Part 3.

 Track 15
Part 4

Look at Part 4, questions 20–25.
There are six sentences for this part.
You will hear a boy called Stewart and his friend Debbie talking about doing a class presentation.
Decide if each sentence is correct or incorrect. If it is correct, tick the box under A for YES. If it is not correct, tick the box under B for NO.
You have 20 seconds to look at the questions for Part 4.

We are now ready to start. Listen carefully. You will hear the recording twice.

Debbie:	So, tomorrow's the big day. I'm feeling … excited. The last time I gave a presentation I really enjoyed it.
Stewart:	I'm a bit nervous, actually. I've never liked standing up in front of the class. Still, I guess it'll be OK.
Debbie:	Yeah, we'll be fine. We know the subject really well, don't we? And we've spent hours doing all that research, and we've practised … I can't remember how many times we've practised. Lots of times, that's for sure.
Stewart:	Debbie, … Do you think we've got enough things to talk about? I mean, Miss Harris said she didn't want us speaking for more than 15 minutes but now … I'm not sure we can talk for that long.
Debbie:	Don't *worry*. We've got plenty of material. And I've managed to find some brilliant photographs we can use for the presentation. I'll put them up on the wall before the class starts.
Stewart:	There's another thing. We need to allow time at the end in case people want to ask us anything, don't we? Do you think we'll be able to answer them?
Debbie:	Yes! Now stop worrying so much! If there are any difficult ones, we can tell people we'll find out after the lesson.
Stewart:	Look, why don't me meet again this evening? We can practise one more time. Just to make sure we get everything perfect.
Debbie:	Um, yeah, it would be a good idea. The problem is I'm going out with some friends this evening. Look, we'll be OK. We can practise tomorrow morning if you want. I'll meet you at school half an hour before the lesson.
Stewart:	That's a good idea. OK. So, see you tomorrow.

Now listen again.

This is the end of Part 4. You now have six minutes to check your answers and copy them on to the answer sheet.

 Track 16

TEST 4   PAPER 2 LISTENING TEST

This is Cambridge English Qualifications B1 Preliminary, Test 4. There are four parts to this test. You will hear each part twice. Before you hear the recording for each part of the test, you will have time to look at the questions. There will also be time for you to check your answers. At the end of the test you will have six minutes to copy your answers onto the answer sheet. The recording will now be stopped. Please ask any questions now, because you are not allowed to speak during the test.

 Track 17

Part 1

Look at part 1. There are seven questions in this part.
For each question, there is a short recording and three pictures.
Choose the correct picture and tick the box below it.
Here is an example:

Narrator: When is the woman getting married?
Man: I've just heard the good news. I hear you're getting married.
Woman: Yes, Peter actually asked me in June but we didn't decide on a date immediately.
Man: So when is the big day?
Woman: Well, we wanted October but we couldn't book the restaurant we liked so now it's November. The thirteenth.

The third picture is correct so there is a tick in box C.
Now look at the three pictures for question 1.

We are now ready to start. Listen carefully. You will hear each recording twice.

1 *Which shop has just opened in town?*

Woman: Now, listeners who live in the area might be interested in the latest addition to the town centre. The high street now has its very own bookshop. You'll find it where the hairdresser's used to be, on the corner. Give them your mobile phone number and they'll send you a text about any new books that arrive.

Now listen again.

2 *Which fruit mustn't the boy eat?*

Boy: Mum? Can I have something to eat?
Woman: It will be dinner soon so I don't want you eating too much. Why don't you have some fruit? There are some apples in the kitchen. Go and get one. You'll see

a box of strawberries out there as well but don't touch them, please. I need them for a cake. Or there are some bananas. Why not eat one of them?

Now listen again.

3 *What is the man doing on Friday?*

Man: Sue, it's Michael here. I'm just calling about this Friday. I've got a meeting at work so I won't be able to meet you. But I'm free on Saturday if you are. I know your car's being repaired but I can always come and get you if you want. Maybe we could go to see that film you were talking about. Call me when you have time.

Now listen again.

4 *What kind of accommodation is the woman living in at the moment?*

Man: Have you moved into your new home yet, Tania?

Woman: Yes, but you wouldn't believe the trouble we had. We sold the flat quickly but we couldn't move into the new house until the building work was finished. We spent three months in a hotel. Anyway, we finally moved into the house last Friday. You must come round and see it.

Now listen again.

5 *Which item(s) is the man selling?*

Woman: Hi Steve. Where are you going?

Man: To the shop. I want to put this notice in their window.

Woman: Hmm, sorry. I can't read it. I haven't got my glasses.

Man: I'm selling something. We bought a rug the other day but decided we don't really like it. I'm hoping somebody might buy it if I put an advert in the shop window. We sold a sofa that way a few weeks ago so maybe we'll be successful again.

Now listen again.

6 *How often does the boy see his grandfather?*

Boy: Are we going to see Grandad soon? We haven't seen him for ages.

Woman: You'd see him every day if you could, wouldn't you? Once a week is enough, though. Grandad likes to see you on Fridays after school. He's busy the rest of the week. And we mustn't forget it's his birthday next month. Any ideas what to get him?

Boy: I'll try and find out what he wants.

Now listen again.

7 *What has the woman forgotten to bring with her?*

Woman: Oh no! Just turn the car round and go back. I've left something at home.

Man: Not the map, I hope. We'll never get there without it.

Woman: No, no, that's on the back seat. I've left my bag on the table.

Man: You don't need it. I've got plenty of money and I've got my phone if you need to call anyone.

Now listen again.

This is the end of Part 1.

 **Track 18**

Part 2

Look at Part 2, questions 8–13.
You will hear part of a radio interview with a woman called Fiona Josephs, who has written a book.
For each question, tick the correct box.
You have 45 seconds to look at the questions for Part 2.

We are now ready to start. Listen carefully. You will hear the recording twice.

Interviewer:	... I'm speaking to Fiona Josephs, who's written a book about a woman called Beatrice Cadbury. Fiona, who was Beatrice?
Fiona:	She came from a famous family who lived in Birmingham. Her father was Richard Cadbury, who started Cadbury's, the company that makes chocolate. Beatrice was a very rich woman but decided to give away all her money to the workers at the Cadbury factory.
Interviewer:	Why did you want to write about her?
Fiona:	Well, one day I was reading about a school in the Netherlands that had been started by a poor married couple – and the wife was called Beatrice Cadbury! I wanted to know if she was a member of the famous Cadbury family. And when I discovered she was, I had lots of questions. Why was a rich woman from Birmingham living as a poor person in the Netherlands? The answer was so amazing that I decided to write a book.
Interviewer:	What did you discover?
Fiona:	Well, she was born in 1884, one of eight children. As a child she lived in huge houses and was educated at the best schools. She had a very comfortable life. But her father wanted to help poor people, people who had very difficult lives. As a result, Beatrice knew how the poor lived and she grew up wanting to make society a better place. She married a man from the Netherlands and left England to begin a new life there with him and their children. While she was in the Netherlands, she decided she didn't want to receive any more money from the Cadbury business. She told her brother, who was running the company, that he should give her share of the money to the factory workers instead. Not surprisingly, her relatives in Birmingham were worried about her and her children.
Interviewer:	And then what happened?
Fiona:	Well, she invited poor people to live in her house. When it became too crowded, she and her family had to live in a tent. However, in later life Beatrice and her husband decided that the best way to change society was through education. They set up a school which became famous. In fact, Queen Beatrix of the Netherlands went there as a child in the 1950s.
Interviewer:	What do you admire most about Beatrice?

Fiona: I admire the fact that she tried to make society a better place, but I can understand why people feel sorry for her children. Even the workers at the factory were unhappy about the way Beatrice was living and didn't want to take her money. But she tried to do good and she thought of others.

Now listen again.

This is the end of Part 2.

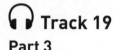 **Track 19**

Part 3

Look at Part 3, questions 14–19.
You will hear a radio announcement about a student film club.
For each question, write the missing information in the numbered space.
You have 20 seconds to look at Part 3.

We are now ready to start. Listen carefully. You will hear the recording twice.

Man: And now it's time to tell all the new students at the university about one of our most popular clubs. The University Film Club is a very friendly and welcoming group of people who meet up regularly to watch some of the latest films as well as some well-known classics from the past. We try to show as wide a variety of films as possible to suit everyone's tastes, including horror, science fiction, romance and thrillers. And if there's a film you'd like to recommend, we're always very happy to hear your suggestions.

Being a member gives you the chance to see films on campus as well as in cinemas in town. Members meet in the lecture theatre in the Education Block, which is just behind the library. Films are shown twice a week on Tuesday and Thursday at 7.00 p.m. and entrance is free to members. We've also managed to agree a discount for film club members with all the main cinemas in town. All members are given 50 per cent off the entry price on any films shown in these cinemas – a great saving if you go to the cinema regularly.

But it's not just about watching films. Once a month we hold a film quiz night. These are always very popular. Other activities include trips to film studios and informal discussions on film-related topics.

At the end of the year members all get together for dinner in town to say goodbye to the students who are leaving the university. And in addition to these activities, you'll often find members deep in discussion in and around the university campus. So if you'd like to increase your circle of friends and have a fantastic social life, the University Film Club is a great choice. It costs just £10 a year to become a member so if you're interested, call Janet on 4358 for more information.

Now listen again.

This is the end of Part 3.

 **Track 20**

Part 4

Look at Part 4, questions 20–25.
Look at the six sentences for this part.
You will hear a man called Don and his wife Angela talking about a family party.
Decide if each sentence is correct or incorrect.
If it is correct, tick (√) the box under A for YES. If it is not correct, tick (√) the box under B for NO.

You have 20 seconds to look at the questions for Part 4.

We are now ready to start. Listen carefully. You will hear the recording twice.

Angela:	OK, I think that's everything. These family parties take a long time to organise, don't they? ... That reminds me. Have you bought the drinks for the children?
Don:	I'm going out later. I'll go to the supermarket on the way home and get some. I don't think we need anything else, do we?
Angela:	Well, I'm not sure we have enough food. You know what my family are like. They always eat everything when they come round.
Don:	Yes, they do eat a lot, but that's OK. I think we've got everything we need.
Angela:	Good! If you could get started with the housework now, I'll get started with the cooking. I don't want to leave everything until the last minute.
Don:	Well, there's isn't much to do, actually. I cleaned and tidied the living room this morning. Oh, and remember you'll have to collect my mum from the station tomorrow. My car's in the garage.
Angela:	Don't worry. I haven't forgotten. Anyway, I'm sure everyone will have a great time. Do you remember last year's party? I burnt the dinner and we had nothing to eat?
Don:	Yes, how could I forget! No, tomorrow, will be just fine. I'm really looking forward to it. It's all the hard work you have to do before that I don't enjoy.
Angela:	Oh, it's fine. It gives us the chance to get the house nice and tidy, and I like deciding what we're going to eat, what I'm going to wear, that kind of thing.
Don:	Maybe. Anyway, I'll start cleaning the dining room.

This is the end of Part 4. You now have six minutes to check your answers and copy them on to the answer sheet.

 **Track 21**

TEST 1   PAPER 3 SPEAKING TEST: MODEL ANSWERS

Part 1: Phase 1

Examiner:	Good morning. Can I have your mark sheets, please? I'm Matthew Humphreys and this is Claire Snow. He's just going to listen to us. Now what's your name?

Candidate A:	Maria. My name is Maria.
Examiner:	Thank you. And what's your name?
Candidate B:	And I'm Manfred.
Examiner:	Thank you. What's your surname?
Candidate B:	Mayr.
Examiner:	How do you spell it?
Candidate B:	M-A-Y-R.
Examiner:	Thank you. And what's your surname?
Candidate A:	Pérez.
Examiner:	How do you write your surname?
Candidate A:	P-E-R-E-Z.
Examiner:	Thank you. Where do you live?
Candidate A:	I live in Madrid.
Examiner:	Do you work or are you a student?
Candidate A:	I'm a school student.
Examiner:	What do you study?
Candidate A:	Well, I study Spanish and also Spanish literature ... other languages are English and French. Also, I study Philosophy and Citizenship, er... let me see, History, Science and Physical Education.
Examiner:	Thank you. And what about you, Manfred? Where do you live?
Candidate B:	I live in Munich.
Examiner:	Do you work or are you a student?
Candidate B:	I'm a student.
Examiner:	And what subjects do you study at school?
Candidate B:	Um ... We have lessons in German, of course, Mathematics, Physics, Chemistry and Biology, History, Politics and Geography. Oh yes! English and Italian. And we also do Religion and Sport.
Examiner:	Thank you.

 Track 22

Part 1: Phase 2

Examiner:	Do you enjoy studying English?
Candidate:	Yes I do. I study English and French and I enjoy learning about different cultures.
Examiner:	Do you think English will be useful for you in the future?
Candidate:	I think so, yes. I'd like to use English for my job and maybe travel to different countries.
Examiner:	What did you do last weekend?
Candidate:	I went shopping with my friends. We live near a big shopping centre and we often go there together.
Examiner:	What do you enjoy doing in your free time?
Candidate:	I like dancing and doing different sports. I also enjoy reading and watching films.

 Track 23

Part 2

Candidate A:	People can do all these things on holiday, can't they? What do you think four friends could do?
Candidate B:	Well, they could do all of these activities. It depends where they're going. If they're staying in a hotel, they could go dancing if the hotel has somewhere that plays music. There's probably a swimming pool or they can go to the beach – they can lie on the beach if they are near the sea. But what do you think is the most fun?
Candidate A:	Let's say what isn't fun first. Looking at a mobile phone or watching TV ... That's not fun, is it? They can do that at home. They should go swimming and walking in the countryside.
Candidate B:	Yes, but I don't think lying on the beach is fun. It's a way to relax, but it's not fun. I think eating different food is the most fun – more fun than walking or taking photos. What do you think?
Candidate A:	I agree. Everybody likes eating, so yes, food or eating is the most fun.

 Track 24

Part 3

Candidate A:	This photograph shows a party at a wedding, a wedding reception. I can see two people only. They're the people who are married. She's the bride and he's the groom. They're quite young, maybe 25 or 30 years old. They're in a room, maybe in a large hotel, but I'm not sure. The bride is wearing a long white dress and she has very long dark hair. The man has a white shirt and black trousers. He isn't wearing a jacket but I think he took this off because it's hot or maybe he doesn't feel comfortable with a jacket and tie. They're cutting the wedding cake ... there are three cakes together. It's traditional to take a photo of this. They're smiling and they look very happy, of course. A wedding is a happy time for everyone. I can't see other people in the photo but I'm sure there are lots of people there.
Candidate B:	My picture also has happy people in it. It's a birthday party. There's some writing behind the people and it says 'Happy birthday'. Most of the people in the photo are women ... nearly all women ... I can only see two men. They're at the back of the group. The ladies are sitting at a table and on the table there are some presents. I can't say what the presents are. They're in bags and boxes, so you can't see them. And I don't know who the party is for ... whose birthday it is. There's a lady – an old lady – she's sitting in the middle, in front of the table. It might be her birthday. Everybody is smiling and looking at the camera. Some of them have something like scarves around their necks ... and they all look happy.

Part 4

Candidate A:	We celebrate the same things in my country: a birthday, a wedding ... When people move to a new house, they sometimes have a party. What do people celebrate in your country?
Candidate B:	The same things, really. I went to a birthday party a little while ago. My friend had a big party with lots of people and lots of food. I enjoyed it.
Candidate A:	Yes, I like birthday parties as well. You see all your relatives: your uncles, aunts and cousins. Sometimes we see people that we haven't seen for a long time. Er ... have you ever been to a wedding?
Candidate B:	Well, I went to a wedding when I was younger but that was a long time ago. I had a birthday party last year. I was 16 and a lot of my friends came. And last week, it was my school prom. My school friends and I all dressed up in our best clothes. Do you have proms in your country?
Candidate A:	Yes, but I haven't had a prom yet. I hope I have a birthday party when I'm 17. I'd like to invite all my friends and relatives, and I hope my parents will pay for everything!

⌒ Track 26

TEST 2   PAPER 3 SPEAKING TEST: MODEL ANSWERS

Part 2

Candidate A:	Shall I start? Well, all these things are useful, aren't they? I think painting is a good idea. It's always nice to paint rooms when you move to a new house, isn't it?
Candidate B:	Yes. We moved house a few months ago and my parents painted the rooms. It's a really quick way of making the house look different. What other things make the house feel like home? ... What about the pictures?
Candidate A:	Well, the pictures are nice but maybe there are other things that are more useful. I don't think the garden is important, not at first, anyway. People can make their gardens look nice later, but furniture is important. When you have your own armchairs and sofas, it feels like home, doesn't it?
Candidate B:	Yes, I agree with you about the furniture. People need to sit down and feel comfortable so I think they need a sofa and some chairs quite soon. And you're right about the garden. They can make that look nice later.
Candidate A:	So. The furniture is one thing. What about the TV? They can sit and watch TV in the evening.
Candidate B:	Yes, the TV is useful as well. I think the house will have a kitchen units so a new kitchen isn't important, not at first, anyway. Do you agree?
Candidate A:	Yes, that can wait. So furniture and a TV first and a nice garden and new kitchen units later.

🎧 Track 27
Part 3

Candidate A: This is a photograph of something that is being built, perhaps a house or a factory. There's a man in the foreground on the left. We can only see his back so I don't know how old he is. He's holding a large piece of paper. I think they're the plans of the building. He's looking at the plans and the building but I don't think he's one of the builders. He's checking that everything is OK ... so I think he's the boss or the manager or he might be the architect. The man's wearing a hat, a safety hat. He's also wearing a warm coat and the sky is cloudy so it's probably cold. The building isn't finished yet. There's a small house in the background and it looks like there's a ... fence on the left but it isn't finished. Perhaps they're building another house. The man is the only person in the photograph. None of the builders can be seen.

Candidate B: This photograph also shows something being made. But the people in the photo are having more fun than the man in the other picture. There are three children in the photo. I think they're three girls but maybe one of them is a boy. It's difficult to see because they're wearing hats. They're standing at a table and they're cooking. Well, they're not cooking yet; they're preparing the food. I think they're making cakes because it looks like they have flour and eggs and they're mixing them together in a bowl. The girl on the left is pouring flour into the bowl. The eggs are already in the bowl and there are egg shells on the table. The other two children are watching the older girl, and I think they're her sisters or her school friends because they're all wearing the same clothes. They all have red aprons with white stripes to keep their clothes clean.

🎧 Track 28
Part 4

Candidate A: I'm like the three children in your photograph: I really enjoy cooking – not only cakes but meals. I've always liked cooking, even when I was a child. Do you like cooking?

Candidate B: I don't cook very often. I still live at home and my parents cook most of the food. But I help them sometimes. I used to be like the children in the picture ... when I was younger ... but not now. Now I like painting and drawing. Is that making things?

Candidate A: Yes, definitely. You're making art. Do you paint often?

Candidate B: I go to art classes once a week, in the evening after school. I can't really paint at home as I don't have enough room in my house and my little brother and sister always want to 'help' me. So it's difficult. Are you a good cook?

Candidate A: I don't know. I usually have to read the instructions in a recipe. But my parents used to ask me to make things when I was younger, not big meals but small things, like snacks for lunch. So I slowly learnt how to do things.

Candidate B: I think I should learn to cook too. It will be useful when I leave home.

 **Track 29**

TEST 3   PAPER 3 SPEAKING TEST: MODEL ANSWERS

Part 2

Candidate A: In my country some libraries are closing because people don't use them so this is quite important. What do you think would make more children visit a library?

Candidate B: Young children need their parents to take them to the library so I think something that makes the parents happy is a good idea. The computers can be used by children *and* parents, can't they?

Candidate A: Yes, that's a good idea. And I think young children like people to read stories for them so maybe somebody who could do this would be a good idea. Now, the CDs. I don't think they're a good way to get children to use the library but in my opinion, computer games would be very popular.

Candidate B: I agree. I don't think CDs would be any good but yes, computer games are good fun. Books ... I don't know ... Everybody knows you get books in a library so I don't think more books would make a library more interesting, do *you*?

Candidate A: No, I don't think so. It must have books but the other things are better ways to get people to use the library. So we think computers and computer games are a good idea. Which ones are the best? I think the computers. What do you think?

Candidate B: I agree. They're useful to both parents and children and especially for people who don't have a computer at home.

 **Track 30**

Part 3

Candidate A: OK. My photograph shows a group of people, well, a family, really, and they're running – jogging. They're jogging in the countryside. There are four people: a father – he's on the left. In front of him is one of the daughters, and then the mother and the other daughter are on the right. The parents look like they're about 30 or 40 and the children ... they look quite young. The girl on the left may be ten. She's older than the girl on the right, I think – she's taller. The man and the younger girl have light brown hair, or maybe it's red, I'm not sure. The mother and the older girl have fair hair. They're all wearing running clothes, tracksuits and trainers and they all look happy. They're smiling and laughing so I think they're enjoying the exercise. Also they're in beautiful countryside. They're jogging along a road and you can see lots of trees behind them and on the side of the road, very green trees. I can't see the sky but I think it's sunny. The weather looks very good.

Candidate B: This photograph shows some children playing football. It's a lovely sunny day and I think they're in a park. There's a building in the background; it might be a school, but I'm not sure. The children are playing football on grass. There are five children: I can see three girls and two boys. They're about eight, nine, or ten years old. I think the boys are playing the girls. I mean, there's a team with boys and a team with girls. The two boys are wearing blue shirts, blue trousers and blue socks, while the three girls are wearing green shirts with red on the side. One of the boys has the football and it looks like one of the girls is trying to stop him. All the children are having fun. It's good to see girls playing football.

 **Track 31**

Part 4

Candidate A:	Would you like to start? Do you do any sport?
Candidate B:	I do sport at school. We have Physical Education two times a week. We do lots of different sports: running, football … We also use the school gym. What about you? Have you got a favourite sport?
Candidate A:	I go running in the morning but my favourite sport is swimming. We have a swimming pool near my apartment and I go there with my friends. One of my friends is a very good swimmer and it was my friend who taught me to swim about five years ago. That's the reason I like it. I can still remember when I couldn't swim.
Candidate B:	Yes, I forgot swimming. That's probably my favourite sport as well. Sometimes I forget swimming is a sport. It's something I do when I feel hot or want to have fun. I don't swim very well but in my country the weather is always warm so it's great to go swimming in a swimming pool or in the sea. … You said you go running. Do you run a long distance?
Candidate A:	Not too long, no. Just a few kilometres. I think it gets boring after a little while. But I love swimming. When did you learn to swim?
Candidate B:	We learnt at school when I was younger. I was probably about five or six. Anyway, so swimming is our favourite sport.

 **Track 32**

TEST 4   PAPER 3 SPEAKING TEST: MODEL ANSWERS

Part 2

Candidate A:	OK. I think if the man is going to university, he'll want to take some of these things, don't you think so? Like the laptop, for example?
Candidate B:	Yes, the laptop is probably the most important thing, but what about the bicycle? If he likes cycling, he'll want his bicycle, won't he? Maybe he can use the computers at the university.
Candidate A:	If he hasn't got much money, he might want to take the TV with him. I know most students have a TV in their room. If he doesn't have one, what will he do in the evening?
Candidate B:	I know. This is difficult, isn't it? Maybe he isn't interested in cycling so we can leave the bicycle. Now what about the radio and the books? I

don't think the radio's important. He can listen to the radio on a laptop. And he'll need to get different books when he arrives at university ... so ... Do you agree he doesn't need to take these things?

Candidate A: Yes, I do. But there's the old toy ... He might feel sad without it but he might feel a little embarrassed if his friends see that he has a toy. So we can take that away. And the iron ... He can borrow an iron. So let's choose the laptop and the TV. Do you think the laptop is best?

Candidate B: Yes. Let's agree on the laptop. He can watch some TV programmes on the laptop and listen to music on it as well and he can use it for work. So the laptop is the best thing to take.

🎧 Track 33
Part 3

Candidate A: This picture shows a family. They're sitting all together in a room. It's a very bright room. There's a big window and the room is very light. There are four people and they're all reading, I think. I can't see what the mother is reading but she's looking down and it looks like she's reading. Her husband is sitting next to her on the sofa. It's a modern sofa with a long white cushion. The man is sitting on her right. He's reading the newspaper. He's wearing glasses ... He's the only one wearing glasses. The parents look quite young, maybe 30 years old, and in front of them are their two children ... two girls. The girls look about eight or nine years old and they're sitting next to each other at a table. They're both laughing so the book might be funny. They all look very relaxed.

Candidate B: Well, I can see a man sitting in a chair with his hands on his head. I think he's at work in his office. He's looking out of the window, a very large window and thinking about something. I can't see his face because he isn't looking towards me. I can only see his back but he looks like he's middle-aged. He has short dark hair and he's wearing a smart shirt. The table is on the right and there are some work things on a very large desk. I can see a computer and I think there's another desk that also has a computer on it ... so yes, the man is definitely in an office. Also on his desk there's some paper and a cup, but it looks very tidy. Outside the window there are a lot of trees. I think the office is very high up. It's a nice photograph and the man is very relaxed.

🎧 Track 34
Part 4

Candidate A: OK, relaxing ... I like to read and watch TV to relax but I like reading best. When I'm reading a good book, I don't think about work or anything else. What about you?

Candidate B: I like watching TV as well but I don't read very much. I like to go walking to relax. I live in the city and I like to walk around the streets. I enjoy looking at the houses or looking in shop windows. It's good exercise and it's interesting as well.

Candidate A: I don't like walking very much. I'm a bit lazy. I like listening to music sometimes, not noisy music but something quiet – slow music. I also like to be alone sometimes. For me it's easier to relax when I'm on my own.

Candidate B: Really? I'm different. I like to be with other people, with good friends. If I know the people, it's easy to relax. I know it isn't so relaxing if you don't know the people very well, though. That can make you a little nervous.

Candidate A: When you work hard, it's difficult to relax in the evening. Maybe you're thinking about your job and what you have to do the next day.

Candidate B: Yes, I agree. So you like reading best to relax and I like walking. Two completely different ways.

CAMBRIDGE ENGLISH
Language Assessment
Part of the University of Cambridge

Candidate Name
If not already printed, write name in CAPITALS and complete the Candidate No. grid (in pencil).

Candidate Signature

Examination Title

Centre

Supervisor:
If the candidate is ABSENT or has WITHDRAWN shade here ▭

Centre No.

Candidate No.

Examination Details

0	0	0	0
1	1	1	1
2	2	2	2
3	3	3	3
4	4	4	4
5	5	5	5
6	6	6	6
7	7	7	7
8	8	8	8
9	9	9	9

PET Paper 1 Reading and Writing Candidate Answer Sheet 1

Instructions

Use a PENCIL (B or HB).

Rub out any answer you want to change with an eraser.

For Reading:
Mark ONE letter for each question.
For example, if you think **A** is the right answer to the question, mark your answer sheet like this:

0	A B C D

Part 1

1	A B C
2	A B C
3	A B C
4	A B C
5	A B C

Part 2

6	A B C D E F G H
7	A B C D E F G H
8	A B C D E F G H
9	A B C D E F G H
10	A B C D E F G H

Part 3

11	A B
12	A B
13	A B
14	A B
15	A B
16	A B
17	A B
18	A B
19	A B
20	A B

Part 4

21	A B C D
22	A B C D
23	A B C D
24	A B C D
25	A B C D

Part 5

26	A B C D
27	A B C D
28	A B C D
29	A B C D
30	A B C D
31	A B C D
32	A B C D
33	A B C D
34	A B C D
35	A B C D

Continue on the other side of this sheet ⟶

denote
Print Limited 0121 520 5100

DP743/389

For **Writing (Parts 1 and 2):**

Write your answers clearly in the spaces provided.

Part 1: Write your answers below.	Do not write here
1	1 1 0
2	1 2 0
3	1 3 0
4	1 4 0
5	1 5 0

Part 2 (Question 6): Write your answer below.

Put your answer to Writing Part 3 on Answer Sheet 2 ➡

Do not write below (Examiner use only)					
0	1	2	3	4	5

CAMBRIDGE ENGLISH
Language Assessment
Part of the University of Cambridge

PRELIMINARY ENGLISH TEST

0090/01

Reading and Writing
ANSWER SHEET 2

Day XX MONTH 201X
Test XXX

* *

Candidate Name

Centre Number

Candidate Number

Answer Sheet for Writing Part 3

INSTRUCTIONS TO CANDIDATES

Write your name, centre number and candidate number in the spaces above.

Write your answer to Writing Part 3 on the other side of this sheet.

You **must** write within the grey lines.

Use a pencil.

Do **not** write on the barcodes.

*

Answer only one of the two questions for Part 3.
Tick the box to show which question you have answered.
Write your answer below. Do not write on the barcodes.

Part 3	Question 7		Question 8	

This section for use by Examiner only:

C	CA	O	L

Candidate Name
If not already printed, write name
in CAPITALS and complete the
Candidate No. grid (in pencil).

Candidate Signature

Examination Title

Centre

Supervisor:
If the candidate is ABSENT or has WITHDRAWN shade here ▭

Centre No.

Candidate No.

Examination Details

PET Paper 2 Listening Candidate Answer Sheet

You must transfer all your answers from the Listening Question Paper to this answer sheet.

Instructions

Use a PENCIL (B or HB).

Rub out any answer you want to change with an eraser.

For **Parts 1, 2** and **4:**
Mark ONE letter for each question.
For example, if you think **A** is the right answer to the
question, mark your answer sheet like this:

For **Part 3:**
Write your answers clearly in the spaces next
to the numbers (14 to 19) like this:

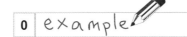

Part 1	Part 2	Part 3		Do not write here	Part 4
1 A B C	8 A B C	14		1 14 0	20 A B
2 A B C	9 A B C	15		1 15 0	21 A B
3 A B C	10 A B C	16		1 16 0	22 A B
4 A B C	11 A B C	17		1 17 0	23 A B
5 A B C	12 A B C	18		1 18 0	24 A B
6 A B C	13 A B C	19		1 19 0	25 A B
7 A B C					

Answer key

TEST 1

Paper 1 Reading and Writing Test

Reading

Part 1

1 B	4 C
2 C	5 A
3 B	

Part 2

6 F	9 B
7 H	10 E
8 C	

Part 3

11 A	16 A
12 B	17 A
13 B	18 B
14 A	19 A
15 B	20 A

Part 4

21 C	24 B
22 B	25 A
23 C	

Part 5

26 A	31 A
27 A	32 C
28 B	33 C
29 C	34 D
30 D	35 B

Writing

Part 1

1 gave him
2 like to
3 enough
4 until
5 forward to going

Paper 2 Listening Test

Part 1

1 C	4 A
2 C	5 B
3 A	6 A
	7 B

Part 2

8 A	11 B
9 B	12 A
10 C	13 B

Part 3

14 galleries	17 14th/14
15 30	18 beginning
16 simple	19 Monday

Part 4

20 A	23 B
21 A	24 A
22 B	25 A

TEST 2

Paper 1 Reading and Writing Test

Reading   ### Writing

Part 1   **Part 1**

1 B   4 B   1 wasn't as
2 A   5 A   2 I would / I'd
3 C   3 to start
                                    4 have not/haven't used / have/'ve never
Part 2   used
6 B   9 C   5 you like
7 D   10 G
8 H   ## Paper 2 Listening Test

Part 3   **Part 1**   4 B
                                    1 B   5 A
11 A   16 B   2 C   6 C
12 B   17 A   3 B   7 A
13 B   18 B
14 A   19 A   **Part 2**
15 B   20 B   8 B   11 C
                                    9 C   12 B
Part 4   10 A   13 A

21 A   24 D   **Part 3**
22 A   25 B
23 B   14 week / Friday   17 DVDs
                                    15 14 / fourteen   18 book
Part 5   16 4.30   19 1457

26 B   31 A   **Part 4**
27 A   32 B
28 D   33 C   20 B   23 B
29 C   34 D   21 A   24 A
30 A   35 A   22 A   25 B

TEST 3

Paper 1 Reading and Writing Test

Reading

Part 1

1 A		**4** B	
2 C		**5** C	
3 B			

Part 2

6 H		**9** A	
7 F		**10** C	
8 E			

Part 3

11 B		**16** B	
12 A		**17** A	
13 A		**18** A	
14 B		**19** B	
15 B		**20** A	

Part 4

21 B		**24** C	
22 B		**25** A	
23 C			

Part 5

26 B		**31** A	
27 D		**32** B	
28 A		**33** D	
29 A		**34** D	
30 C		**35** C	

Writing

Part 1

1 such a
2 far from
3 since
4 not to take
5 faster than

Paper 2 Listening Test

Part 1

1 C		**4** C	
2 B		**5** B	
3 C		**6** A	
		7 A	

Part 2

8 C		**11** B	
9 B		**12** C	
10 A		**13** A	

Part 3

14 snacks		**17** 6 / six	
15 warm		**18** July	
16 website		**19** entrance	

Part 4

20 B		**23** B	
21 A		**24** A	
22 A		**25** A	

TEST 4

Paper 1 Reading and Writing Test

Reading

Part 1

1	C	**4**	C
2	A	**5**	B
3	C		

Part 2

6	G	**9**	A
7	E	**10**	H
8	C		

Part 3

11	B	**16**	B
12	A	**17**	B
13	A	**18**	B
14	B	**19**	A
15	A	**20**	B

Part 4

21	A	**24**	D
22	C	**25**	B
23	A		

Part 5

26	C	**31**	D
27	A	**32**	A
28	D	**33**	C
29	B	**34**	A
30	B	**35**	B

Writing

Part 1

1 were you
2 many / a lot of / lots of
3 It has / It's
4 waiting
5 was given

Paper 2 Listening Test

Part 1

1	B	**4**	C
2	C	**5**	C
3	A	**6**	B
		7	B

Part 2

8	B	**11**	A
9	A	**12**	B
10	C	**13**	C

Part 3

14	thrillers	**17**	quiz (night)
15	Education	**18**	dinner
16	free	**19**	4358

Part 4

20	B	**23**	B
21	A	**24**	A
22	B	**25**	A

FRAMEWORK FOR PAPER 3 SPEAKING TEST

Below are examples of what the examiner might say in each part of the Speaking test and the questions he/she might ask. It is important to familiarise yourself with the 'framework' for the Speaking test as this will help you understand what is expected of you. Make sure you learn good responses for Phase 1 of Part 1.

TEST 1

Part 1   (2–3 minutes)
Phase 1

Examiner: (to Candidates A and B)

Good morning/afternoon/evening.
Can I have your mark sheets please?

I'm ... and this is ... .
He/She is just going to listen to us.

Examiner: (to Candidate A)

Now what's your name?
Thank you.

Examiner: (to Candidate B)

And what's your name?
Thank you.
What's your surname?
How do you spell it?
Thank you.

Examiner: (to Candidate A)

And what's your surname?
How do you write your surname?
Thank you.

Examiner: (possible questions to both candidates)

- Where do you live?
- Do you work or are you a student?
- What job do you do?/What do you study?
Thank you.

Phase 2

Examiner: (possible questions to both candidates)
- Do you enjoy studying English?
- Do you think English will be useful for you in the future?
- What did you do last weekend?
- What do you enjoy doing in your free time?

Thank you.

In the next part, you are going to talk to each other.

Part 2 (2–3 minutes)

Examiner: I'm going to describe a situation to you.

Four friends are going on holiday in the summer.

Talk together about the things they could do on their holiday and which things would be the most fun.

Here is a picture with some ideas to help you.

Look at the image on page i of the colour supplement.

I'll say that again.

Four friends are going on holiday in the summer.

Talk together about the things they could do on their holiday and which things would be the most fun.

All right? Talk together.

Part 3   (3 minutes)

FAMILY CELEBRATIONS

Examiner: Now I'd like each of you to talk on your own about something.
I'm going to give each of you a photograph of people at a family
celebration.

Candidate A, here is your photograph.
Look at the image on page ii of the colour supplement.
Please show it to Candidate B but I'd like you to talk about it.
Candidate B, you just listen. I'll give you your photograph in a minute.
Candidate A, please tell us what you can see in the photograph.

Examiner: Now, Candidate B, here is your photograph.
Look at the image on page ii of the colour supplement.
It also shows people at a family celebration.
Please show it to Candidate A and tell us what you can see in the
photograph.

Part 4   (3 minutes)

Examiner: Your photographs showed families celebrating something.
Now I'd like you to talk about which things families celebrate
in your country.

Thank you. That's the end of the test.

TEST 2

Part 1   (2–3 minutes)

Phase 1

Examiner: (to Candidates A and B)

> Good morning/afternoon/evening.
> Can I have your mark sheets please?
>
> I'm ... and this is ... .
> He/She is just going to listen to us.

Examiner: (to Candidate A)

> Now what's your name?
> Thank you.

Examiner: (to Candidate B)

> And what's your name?
> Thank you.
> What's your surname?
> How do you spell it?
> Thank you.

Examiner: (to Candidate A)

> And what's your surname?
> How do you write your surname?
> Thank you.

Examiner: (possible questions to both candidates)

> - Where do you live?
> - Do you work or are you a student?
> - What job do you do?/What do you study?
> Thank you.

Phase 2

Examiner: (possible questions to both candidates)

> - Can you tell me something about your family?
> - Do you spend a lot of time with your family?
> - Do you have a pet?
> - Tell me something about your pet./Would you like to have a pet?
> Thank you.
>
> In the next part, you are going to talk to each other.

Part 2 (2–3 minutes)

Examiner: I'm going to describe a situation to you.
A couple have just moved into a new house.
Talk together about the things they could do to the house immediately to make it feel like home and which things they could do later.

Here is a picture with some ideas to help you.
Look at the image on page iii of the colour supplement.

I'll say that again.
A couple have just moved into a new house.
Talk together about the things she could do to the house immediately to make it feel like home and which things they could do later.

All right? Talk together.

Part 3   (3 minutes)

MAKING THINGS

Examiner: Now I'd like each of you to talk on your own about something.
I'm going to give each of you a photograph of people making things.

Candidate A, here is your photograph.
Look at the image on page iv of the colour supplement.
Please show it to Candidate B but I'd like you to talk about it.
Candidate B, you just listen. I'll give you your photograph in a minute.
Candidate A, please tell us what you can see in the photograph.

Examiner: Now, Candidate B, here is your photograph.
Look at the image on page iv of the colour supplement.
It also shows people making things.
Please show it to Candidate A and tell us what you can see in the
photograph.

Part 4   (3 minutes)

Examiner: Your photographs showed people making things.
Now I'd like you to talk about what kind of things you liked to make when
you were younger and what things you like to make now.

Thank you. That's the end of the test.

TEST 3

Part 1   (2–3 minutes)
Phase 1

Examiner: (to Candidates A and B)

Good morning/afternoon/evening.
Can I have your mark sheets please?

I'm ... and this is ... .
He/She is just going to listen to us.

Examiner: (to Candidate A)

Now what's your name?
Thank you.

Examiner: (to Candidate B)

And what's your name?
Thank you.
What's your surname?
How do you spell it?
Thank you.

Examiner: (to Candidate A)

And what's your surname?
How do you write your surname?
Thank you.

Examiner: (possible questions to both candidates)

• Where do you live?
• Do you work or are you a student?
• What job do you do?/What do you study?
Thank you.

Phase 2

Examiner: (possible questions to both candidates)

• Do you live in a house or a flat?
• Can you tell me something about the area you live in?
• Do you like the area where you live? Why/Why not?
Thank you.

In the next part, you are going to talk to each other.

Part 2 (2–3 minutes)

Examiner: I'm going to describe a situation to you.
A library wants to encourage more children to use it.
Talk together about the things it could do to get children to use the library and which idea would be best.

Here is a picture with some ideas to help you.
Look at the image on page v of the colour supplement.

I'll say that again.
A library wants to encourage more children to use it.
Talk together about the things it could do to get children to use the library and which idea would be best.

All right? Talk together.

Part 3   (3 minutes)

DOING SPORT

Examiner: Now I'd like each of you to talk on your own about something.
            I'm going to give each of you a photograph showing people enjoying sport.
            Candidate A, here is your photograph.
            Look at the image on page vi of the colour supplement.
            Please show it to Candidate B but I'd like you to talk about it.
            Candidate B, you just listen. I'll give you your photograph in a minute.
            Candidate A, please tell us what you can see in the photograph.

Examiner: Now, Candidate B, here is your photograph.
            Look at the image on page vi of the colour supplement.
            It also shows people enjoying sport. Please show it to Candidate A and tell
            us what you can see in the photograph.

Part 4   (3 minutes)

Examiner: Your photographs showed people doing a sport. Now I'd like you to talk
            about what kind of sports you like to do and say why you like them.

            Thank you. That's the end of the test.

TEST 4

Part 1   (2–3 minutes)
Phase 1

Examiner: (to Candidates A and B)

Good morning/afternoon/evening.
Can I have your mark sheets please?

I'm ... and this is ... .
He/She is just going to listen to us.

Examiner: (to Candidate A)

Now what's your name?
Thank you.

Examiner: (to Candidate B)

And what's your name?
Thank you.
What's your surname?
How do you spell it?
Thank you.

Examiner: (to Candidate A)

And what's your surname?
How do you write your surname?
Thank you.

Examiner: (possible questions to both candidates)

- Where do you live?
- Do you work or are you a student?
- What job do you do?/What do you study?
Thank you.

Phase 2

Examiner:
- Do you enjoy watching TV?
- What programmes do you watch?
- Do you like going to the cinema or do you prefer doing other things in your free time?
- Do you spend a lot of time in front of a computer?
Thank you.

In the next part, you are going to talk to each other.

Part 2   (2–3 minutes)

Examiner: I'm going to describe a situation to you.
A young man is leaving home to study at university.
Talk together about the things he should take with him and which thing
would be the most useful.

Here is a picture with some ideas to help you.
Look at the image on page vii of the colour supplement.

I'll say that again.
A young man is leaving home to study at university.
Talk together about the things he should take with him and which thing
would be the most useful.

All right? Talk together.

Part 3   (3 minutes)

RELAXING

Examiner: Now I'd like each of you to talk on your own about something. I'm going to give each of you a photograph showing people relaxing.

Candidate A, here is your photograph.
Look at the image on page viii of the colour supplement.
Please show it to Candidate B but I'd like you to talk about it.
Candidate B, you just listen. I'll give you your photograph in a minute.
Candidate A, please tell us what you can see in the photograph.

Examiner: Now, Candidate B, here is your photograph.
Look at the image on page viii of the colour supplement.
It also shows people at a family celebration. Please show it to Candidate A and tell us what you can see in the photograph.

Part 4   (3 minutes)

Examiner: Your photographs showed people relaxing. Now I'd like you to talk about what kind of things you like to do to relax.

Thank you. That's the end of the test.

Speaking: model answers

TEST 1

Part 1   Phase 1

21

Examiner:	Good morning. Can I have your mark sheets, please? I'm Claire Humphreys and this is Matthew Snow. He's just going to listen to us. Now what's your name?
Candidate A:	Maria. My name is Maria.
Examiner:	Thank you. And what's your name?
Candidate B:	And I'm Manfred.
Examiner:	Thank you. What's your surname?
Candidate B:	Mayr.
Examiner:	How do you spell it?
Candidate B:	M-A-Y-R.
Examiner:	Thank you. And what's your surname?
Candidate A:	Pérez.
Examiner:	How do you write your surname?
Candidate A:	P-E-R-E-Z.
Examiner:	Thank you. Where do you live?
Candidate A:	I live in Madrid.
Examiner:	Do you work or are you a student?
Candidate A:	I'm a school student.
Examiner:	What do you study?
Candidate A:	Well, I study Spanish and also Spanish literature ... other languages are English and French. Also, I study Philosophy and Citizenship, er... let me see, History, Science and Physical Education.
Examiner:	Thank you. And what about you, Manfred? Where do you live?
Candidate B:	I live in Munich.
Examiner:	Do you work or are you a student?
Candidate B:	I'm a student.
Examiner:	And what subjects do you study at school?
Candidate B:	Um ... We have lessons in German, of course, Mathematics, Physics, Chemistry and Biology, History, Politics and Geography. Oh yes! English and Italian. And we also do Religion and Sport.
Examiner:	Thank you.

Part 1   Phase 2

22

Examiner:	Do you enjoy studying English?
Candidate:	Yes I do. I study English and French and I enjoy learning about different cultures.
Examiner:	Do you think English will be useful for you in the future?
Candidate:	I think so, yes. I'd like to use English for my job and maybe travel to different countries.

Examiner:	What did you do last weekend?
Candidate:	I went shopping with my friends. We live near a big shopping centre and we often go there together.
Examiner:	What do you enjoy doing in your free time?
Candidate:	I like dancing and doing different sports. I also enjoy reading and watching films.

Part 2

23

Candidate A:	People can do all these things on holiday, can't they? What do you think four friends could do?
Candidate B:	Well, they could do all of these activities. It depends where they're going. If they're staying in a hotel, they could go dancing if the hotel has somewhere that plays music. There's probably a swimming pool or they can go to the beach – they can lie on the beach if they are near the sea. But what do you think is the most fun?
Candidate A:	Let's say what isn't fun first. Looking at a mobile phone or watching TV ... That's not fun, is it? They can do that at home. They should go swimming and walking in the countryside.
Candidate B:	Yes, but I don't think lying on the beach is fun. It's a way to relax, but it's not fun. I think eating different food is the most fun – more fun than walking or taking photos. What do you think?
Candidate A:	I agree. Everybody likes eating, so yes, food or eating is the most fun.

Part 3

24

Candidate A:	This photograph shows a party at a wedding, a wedding reception. I can see two people only. They're the people who are married. She's the bride and he's the groom. They're quite young, maybe 25 or 30 years old. They're in a room, maybe in a large hotel, but I'm not sure. The bride is wearing a long white dress and she has very long dark hair. The man has a white shirt and black trousers. He isn't wearing a jacket but I think he took this off because it's hot or maybe he doesn't feel comfortable with a jacket and tie. They're cutting the wedding cake ... there are three cakes together. It's traditional to take a photo of this. They're smiling and they look very happy, of course. A wedding is a happy time for everyone. I can't see other people in the photo but I'm sure there are lots of people there.
Candidate B:	My picture also has happy people in it. It's a birthday party. There's some writing behind the people and it says 'Happy birthday'. Most of the people in the photo are women ... nearly all women ... I can only see two men. They're at the back of the group. The ladies are sitting at a table and on the table there are some presents. I can't say what the presents are. They're in bags and boxes, so you can't see them. And I don't know who the party is for ... whose birthday it is. There's a lady – an old lady – she's

sitting in the middle, in front of the table. It might be her birthday. Everybody is smiling and looking at the camera. Some of them have something like scarves around their necks ... and they all look happy.

Part 4

Candidate A: We celebrate the same things in my country: a birthday, a wedding ... When people move to a new house, they sometimes have a party. What do people celebrate in your country?

Candidate B: The same things, really. I went to a birthday party a little while ago. My friend had a big party with lots of people and lots of food. I enjoyed it.

Candidate A: Yes, I like birthday parties as well. You see all your relatives: your uncles, aunts and cousins. Sometimes we see people that we haven't seen for a long time. Er ... have you ever been to a wedding?

Candidate B: Well, I went to a wedding when I was younger but that was a long time ago. I had a birthday party last year. I was 16 and a lot of my friends came. And last week, it was my school prom. My school friends and I all dressed up in our best clothes. Do you have proms in your country?

Candidate A: Yes, but I haven't had a prom yet. I hope I have a birthday party when I'm 17. I'd like to invite all my friends and relatives, and I hope my parents will pay for everything!

TEST 2

Part 1

See model answer for Part 1 in Test 1 on page 162.

Part 2

Candidate A: Shall I start? Well, all these things are useful, aren't they? I think painting is a good idea. It's always nice to paint rooms when you move to a new house, isn't it?

Candidate B: Yes. We moved house a few months ago and my parents painted the rooms. It's a really quick way of making the house look different. What other things make the house feel like home? ... What about the pictures?

Candidate A: Well, the pictures are nice but maybe there are other things that are more useful. I don't think the garden is important, not at first, anyway. People can make their gardens look nice later, but furniture is important. When you have your own armchairs and sofas, it feels like home, doesn't it?

Candidate B: Yes, I agree with you about the furniture. People need to sit down and feel comfortable so I think they need a sofa and some chairs quite soon. And you're right about the garden. They can make that look nice later.

Candidate A:	So. The furniture is one thing. What about the TV? They can sit and watch TV in the evening.
Candidate B:	Yes, the TV is useful as well. I think the house will have kitchen units so a new kitchen isn't important, not at first, anyway. Do you agree?
Candidate A:	Yes, that can wait. So furniture and a TV first and a nice garden and new kitchen units later.

Part 3

Candidate A:	This is a photograph of something that is being built, perhaps a house or a factory. There's a man in the foreground on the left. We can only see his back so I don't know how old he is. He's holding a large piece of paper. I think they're the plans of the building. He's looking at the plans and the building but I don't think he's one of the builders. He's checking that everything is OK ... so I think he's the boss or the manager or he might be the architect. The man's wearing a hat, a safety hat. He's also wearing a warm coat and the sky is cloudy so it's probably cold. The building isn't finished yet. There's a small house in the background and it looks like there's a ... fence on the left but it isn't finished. Perhaps they're building another house. The man is the only person in the photograph. None of the builders can be seen.
Candidate B:	This photograph also shows something being made. But the people in the photo are having more fun than the man in the other picture. There are three children in the photo. I think they're three girls but maybe one of them is a boy. It's difficult to see because they're wearing hats. They're standing at a table and they're cooking. Well, they're not cooking yet; they're preparing the food. I think they're making cakes because it looks like they have flour and eggs and they're mixing them together in a bowl. The girl on the left is pouring flour into the bowl. The eggs are already in the bowl and there are egg shells on the table. The other two children are watching the older girl, and I think they're her sisters or her school friends because they're all wearing the same clothes. They all have red aprons with white stripes to keep their clothes clean.

Part 4

Candidate A:	I'm like the three children in your photograph: I really enjoy cooking – not only cakes but meals. I've always liked cooking, even when I was a child. Do *you* like cooking?
Candidate B:	I don't cook very often. I still live at home and my parents cook most of the food. But I help them sometimes. I used to be like the children in the picture ... when I was younger ... but not now. Now I like painting and drawing. Is that making things?
Candidate A:	Yes, definitely. You're making art. Do you paint often?

Candidate B:	I go to art classes once a week, in the evening after school. I can't really paint at home as I don't have enough room in my house and my little brother and sister always want to 'help' me. So it's difficult. Are you a good cook?
Candidate A:	I don't know. I usually have to read the instructions in a recipe. But my parents used to ask me to make things when I was younger, not big meals but small things, like snacks for lunch. So I slowly learnt how to do things.
Candidate B:	I think I should learn to cook too. It will be useful when I leave home.

TEST 3

Part 1

See model answer for Part 1 in Test 1 on page 162.

Part 2

29

Candidate A:	In my country some libraries are closing because people don't use them so this is quite important. What do you think would make more children visit a library?
Candidate B:	Young children need their parents to take them to the library so I think something that makes the parents happy is a good idea. The computers can be used by children *and* parents, can't they?
Candidate A:	Yes, that's a good idea. And I think young children like people to read stories for them so maybe somebody who could do this would be a good idea. Now, the CDs. I don't think they're a good way to get children to use the library but in my opinion, computer games would be very popular.
Candidate B:	I agree. I don't think CDs would be any good but yes, computer games are good fun. Books ... I don't know ... Everybody knows you get books in a library so I don't think more books would make a library more interesting, do *you?*
Candidate A:	No, I don't think so. It must have books but the other things are better ways to get people to use the library. So we think computers and computer games are a good idea. Which ones are the best? I think the computers. What do you think?
Candidate B:	I agree. They're useful to both parents and children and especially for people who don't have a computer at home.

Part 3

30

| Candidate A: | OK. My photograph shows a group of people, well, a family, really, and they're running – jogging. They're jogging in the countryside. There are four people: a father – he's on the left. In front of him is one of the daughters, and then the mother and the other daughter are on the right. The parents look like they're about 30 or 40 and the children ... they look quite young. The girl on the left may be ten. She's older than |

the girl on the right, I think – she's taller. The man and the younger girl have light brown hair, or maybe it's red, I'm not sure. The mother and the older girl have fair hair. They're all wearing running clothes, tracksuits and trainers and they all look happy. They're smiling and laughing so I think they're enjoying the exercise. Also they're in beautiful countryside. They're jogging along a road and you can see lots of trees behind them and on the side of the road, very green trees. I can't see the sky but I think it's sunny. The weather looks very good.

Candidate B: This photograph shows some children playing football. It's a lovely sunny day and I think they're in a park. There's a building in the background; it might be a school, but I'm not sure. The children are playing football on grass. There are five children: I can see three girls and two boys. They're about eight, nine, or ten years old. I think the boys are playing the girls. I mean, there's a team with boys and a team with girls. The two boys are wearing blue shirts, blue trousers and blue socks, while the three girls are wearing green shirts with red on the side. One of the boys has the football and it looks like one of the girls is trying to stop him. All the children are having fun. It's good to see girls playing football.

Part 4

Candidate A: Would you like to start? Do you do any sport?

Candidate B: I do sport at school. We have physical education two times a week. We do lots of different sports: running, football … We also use the school gym. What about you? Have you got a favourite sport?

Candidate A: I go running in the morning but my favourite sport is swimming. We have a swimming pool near my apartment and I go there with my friends. One of my friends is a very good swimmer and it was my friend who taught me to swim about five years ago. That's the reason I like it. I can still remember when I couldn't swim.

Candidate B: Yes, I forgot swimming. That's probably my favourite sport as well. Sometimes I forget swimming is a sport. It's something I do when I feel hot or want to have fun. I don't swim very well but in my country the weather is always warm so it's great to go swimming in a swimming pool or in the sea. … You said you go running. Do you run a long distance?

Candidate A: Not too long, no. Just a few kilometres. I think it gets boring after a little while. But I love swimming. When did you learn to swim?

Candidate B: We learnt at school when I was younger. I was probably about five or six. Anyway, so swimming is our favourite sport.

TEST 4

Part 1

See model answer for Part 1 in Test 1 on page 162.

Part 2

32

Candidate A: OK. I think if the man is going to university, he'll want to take some of these things, don't you think so? Like the laptop, for example?

Candidate B: Yes, the laptop is probably the most important thing, but what about the bicycle? If he likes cycling, he'll want his bicycle, won't he? Maybe he can use the computers at the university.

Candidate A: If he hasn't got much money, he might want to take the TV with him. I know most students have a TV in their room. If he doesn't have one, what will he do in the evening?

Candidate B: I know. This is difficult, isn't it? Maybe he isn't interested in cycling so we can leave the bicycle. Now what about the radio and the books? I don't think the radio's important. He can listen to the radio on a laptop. And he'll need to get different books when he arrives at university ... so ... Do you agree he doesn't need to take these things?

Candidate A: Yes, I do. But there's the old toy ... He might feel sad without it but he might feel a little embarrassed if his friends see that he has a toy. So we can take that away. And the iron ... He can borrow an iron. So let's choose the laptop and the TV. Do you think the laptop is best?

Candidate B: Yes. Let's agree on the laptop. He can watch some TV programmes on the laptop and listen to music on it as well and he can use it for work. So the laptop is the best thing to take.

Part 3

33

Candidate A: This picture shows a family. They're sitting all together in a room. It's a very bright room. There's a big window and the room is very light. There are four people and they're all reading, I think. I can't see what the mother is reading but she's looking down and it looks like she's reading. Her husband is sitting next to her on the sofa. It's a modern sofa with a long white cushion. The man is sitting on her right. He's reading the newspaper. He's wearing glasses ... He's the only one wearing glasses. The parents look quite young, maybe 20 or 30 years old, and in front of them are their two children ... two girls. The girls look about eight or nine years old and they're sitting next to each other at a table. They're both laughing so the book might be funny. They all look very relaxed.

Candidate B: Well, I can see a man sitting in a chair with his hands on his head. I think he's at work in his office. He's looking out of the window, a very large window and thinking about something. I can't see his face because he isn't looking towards me. I can only see his back but he looks like he's middle-aged. He has short dark hair and he's wearing a smart shirt. The table is on the right and there are some work things on a very large desk. I can see a computer and I think there's another desk that also has a computer on it ... so yes, the man is definitely in an office. Also on his desk there's some paper and a cup, but it looks very tidy. Outside the window there are a lot of trees. I think the office is very high up. It's a nice photograph and the man is very relaxed.

Part 4

Candidate A:	OK, relaxing ... I like to read and watch TV to relax but I like reading best. When I'm reading a good book, I don't think about work or anything else. What about you?
Candidate B:	I like watching TV as well but I don't read very much. I like to go walking to relax. I live in the city and I like to walk around the streets. I enjoy looking at the houses or looking in shop windows. It's good exercise and it's interesting as well.
Candidate A:	I don't like walking very much. I'm a bit lazy. I like listening to music sometimes, not noisy music but something quiet – slow music. I also like to be alone sometimes. For me it's easier to relax when I'm on my own.
Candidate B:	Really? I'm different. I like to be with other people, with good friends. If I know the people, it's easy to relax. I know it isn't so relaxing if you don't know the people very well, though. That can make you a little nervous.
Candidate A:	When you work hard, it's difficult to relax in the evening. Maybe you're thinking about your job and what you have to do the next day.
Candidate B:	Yes, I agree. So you like reading best to relax and I like walking. Two completely different ways.

Writing: model answers

TEST 1

Part 2

Hi Sarah

Thanks for your email! I hope your exam results are great when they arrive. It was really nice of you to invite me to your party. Do you want me to bring anything like drinks or cakes?

Pierre

Part 3

Dear Carla

It was great to hear from you! I'd be happy to help you with your project. I usually eat something simple like cereal during the week because I don't have much time in the morning to cook anything. My brother is always in a hurry in the morning so he just has a slice of toast. I think most people have a breakfast like this. They also usually drink a cup of coffee to help them wake up but I prefer fruit juice. On Saturdays we have more time in the mornings so we have a cooked breakfast with eggs and baked beans.

Write back soon!

Maria

The knock at the door

It was early in the morning when I heard the knock at the door. The noise woke me. I got up and quickly put some clothes on. Then I walked to the window to see who was visiting me at that hour. I looked down and saw a man standing at the front door. He was carrying something and looking at his watch. I didn't recognise him and as I went downstairs, I felt a little scared. I opened the door nervously and said: 'Can I help you?' 'Your pizza, sir,' he replied. 'Sorry I'm so late.'

TEST 2

Part 2

Hi Margaret

I hope you're well. Guess what! I'm doing art classes at a college near my house. We're learning how to draw and paint. I've always enjoyed drawing but now I want to be better and learn new skills. That's why I decided to do this course.

Carlos

Part 3

Dear Mark

Many thanks for your letter. I hope you and your family are well. It's great to hear your parents want a pet. I think dogs make the best pets. They give you so much love and they also help you keep fit – you have to take them out for long walks every day! If you want a pet that's more independent, a cat is better. And remember, if you go on holiday, you'll have to think about what you're going to do with your pet – you'll need to find someone to look after it.

Write back soon!

Lucy

The lights went out

What a lovely evening it was! My boyfriend and I were celebrating our anniversary in a restaurant near my home and we were enjoying some wonderful Chinese food.

Suddenly, the room went dark. There was a problem with the electricity supply and none of the lights were working. The waiter quickly came over and put candles on everyone's table, which made the room look really beautiful.

We have never forgotten that evening. It was probably the most romantic meal we have ever had and we sometimes put candles on the dinner table to remember it.

TEST 3

Part 2

> *Hi Ellen*
>
> *How are you? I'm really enjoying my Spanish course. I've just bought some text books from an online bookshop. Our teacher told us we needed them to practise grammar and vocabulary and also to prepare for our exams.*
>
> *Sally*

Part 3

> *Dear Cameron*
>
> *Thank you for your letter! Are you very excited about living in a new apartment? To answer your questions, I live with my parents and my brother in a house in Paris. We've lived here since I was born. It's a small house with a garden and it's close to the city centre. I can walk to the shops in about five minutes. I like our house because I have a big bedroom and lots of space to keep my things. It's also nice to sit in the garden when the sun shines.*
>
> *Write back soon!*
>
> *Roberto*

> *When the phone rang, I knew who it was. I went to the phone and picked it up. 'Hello, is that Paula?' I said. Paula was my best friend and she was coming home after a long holiday. I hadn't seen her for three months. She told me she was at the airport and asked me to collect her. 'Of course,' I said. I ran to my car and drove to the airport. About one hour later I was standing in Arrivals and Paula was waiting for me. It was great to see my best friend again.*

TEST 4

Part 2

Dear Jane

Thanks for your kind invitation! Unfortunately, I can't come to your party. I have an English exam the next day and I need to study in the evening. I want to get you a present so please write and tell me what you'd like.

Sophia

Part 3

Dear Hugh

Thank you for your letter. I hope the weather is nice for your camping holiday. I've never been camping before. Is it good fun? This year I'm going on holiday with my parents and my brother. We're going to a village near the sea. We usually stay in a rented house or cottage. We usually go to places in my own country because my mother doesn't like travelling by plane. The weather here isn't very good so I prefer going somewhere near a shopping centre. Then if it rains, I can go shopping!

Write back soon!

Mark

A strange noise

I woke up in the morning and I picked up my mobile phone to see if I had any messages. I was reading a text message when I heard a noise. It was a strange noise and it sounded like somebody playing with paper. I got out of bed and looked under the bed and in the wardrobe but I couldn't see anything. Then I opened my bedroom door and looked in the next room. What a surprise! There was a bird flying around the room. The window was open and the bird had flown into the bedroom!

Collins Connect

Accessing the online training module

The Collins practice tests book for *Cambridge English Qualifications B1 Preliminary* gives you access to a free online training module to help prepare you for the test.

> To access the training module go to www.connect.collins.co.uk/ELT and follow the instructions.
>
> The access code is
>
> **4986PET**

If you need any help with registering on Collins Connect, please contact us on

education.support@harpercollins.co.uk